Bio

BRIAN MENDLER

Plagued by severe undiagnosed ADHD and reading difficulties, I began disrupting class in 4th grade. I called teachers names, flipped over desks, and loved to break rules. I was kicked out of school in the middle of 6th grade and sent to a private school. During my senior year, I started gambling. The next five years were a blur of late nights at the casino, thousands of lost dollars, and indescribable misery. Finally, I entered gamblers anonymous and have been clean for 12 years. I have my masters in elementary and special education. I am a successful teacher, adjunct professor and volunteer with Big Brothers/Big Sisters and Special Olympics. I am the co-author and author of three books, including national best seller, *Discipline with Dignity 3rd Edition, Strategies for Successful Classroom Management* and *The Taming of the Crew.* I provide staff development training in a high energy, strategy soaked forum where you will laugh, cry, and walk away believing that every student can and will be successful.

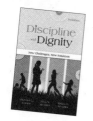

The Teacher Learning Center is proud to provide exceptional staff development services in the areas of classroom management, discipline, and student motivation to school districts all over the world.

You can follow **Brian's blog**: www.Brianmendler.com
You can also follow him on **Twitter**: @BrianMendler

To contact Brian for keynote, on-site training, institutes, and/ or webinars call 1-800-772-5227.

Printed in the United States of America.
Design by Blue Water Printing, Rochester, NY

ISBN 978-1-4951-2185-2

Dedication

To my children: *Elijah Michael Mendler and Brooklyn Rose Mendler. Dada is so proud of you.*

And to my wife, Renee: *Your love, guidance, patience, support, friendship, and dedication to our children and our family continue to make me a better person. I am so lucky to have you by my side. I love you.*

Acknowledgements

I am so grateful to my business partner, Jon Crabbe, and our staff at the Teacher Learning Center and Yolickity, Frozen Yogurt Bar. Allison Yauchzee, Elizabeth Sherwood, and Erin Lamp. Your expertise, professionalism, and dedication to our company are always appreciated.

It is rare in life for a person's father to be their mentor, role-model, and best friend. Allen Mendler is all three. Thank you for all the doors you have opened. I am honored to follow in your footsteps.

My mom, Barbara Mendler, spent hours editing this book. I continue to learn from her every day. Thanks for being the best mom and grandmother a person could ask for.

A few years ago my brother Jason, his wife Ticia, and their kids; Caleb, Ava, and Megan moved from Columbus, OH back to Rochester, NY primarily so our kids could grow up together. I cannot explain in words how much that meant to our family. Your kids are my kid's life. I will always appreciate you putting family first. We love you.

I am so proud of my sister Lisa and brother-in-law Zach. Lisa is a fantastic young educator at a very difficult school in New York City. I am amazed by your accomplishments and look forward to watching your continued journey through education.

To my entire staff at Yolickity, thank you for all your hard work and dedication to our business. I am grateful to each of you.

To all members of my Monday night meeting: Without you none of this is possible. "Keep coming back it works if you work it you're worth it so work it."

I would also like to acknowledge the following educators for the passion, devotion, and dedication they continue to show their students. Thank you.

Nancy	Adair	Teacher	Waverly-South Shore	South Dakota
Greg	Annoni	Assistant Principal	Macungie	Pennsylvania
Debbie	Baldwin	Teacher	Joliet	Illinois
Toni	Barber	Teacher	Holley	New York
Roxana	Betancourt	Teacher	Harlingen	Texas
Peter	Boland	Teacher		Rhode Island
Michelle L.	Boyd	Teacher	War	West Virginia
LaWanna	Brown	Teacher	Dublin	Georgia
Jennifer	Burns	Teacher	Watertown	South Dakota
Bridget	Byers Foes	Special Education Coordinator	Princeton	Illinois
John	Campbell	Assistant Principal	Omaha	Nebraska
Liz	Carrera Cox	Teacher	Joliet	Illinois

Angela	Chase	Teacher	Frederick	Maryland
Brenda	Cole-Carroll	Teacher	Carrollton	Kentucky
Kelly	Creighton Holmes	Teacher	Morrisville	New York
Donna	Cruise	Teacher	Bluefield	West Virginia
Michelle	Cullen	Teacher	Joliet	Illinois
Charla	Danelle Perry	Teacher	Carrollton	Kentucky
Janice	Darif	New Teacher Mentor	Joliet	Illinois
Amy	Dasinger	Teacher	Perry	Ohio
Bridget	DeMarse Dundon	Teacher	La Fargeville	New York
Jeremy	Devine	Teacher	Grand Forks	North Dakota
Jennifer	Drake	Teacher	Rochester	New York
Becky	Dunham	Teacher	Pontiac	Illinois
Michelle	Dykstra Dahl	Teacher	New Lenox	Illinois
Beth	Espinosa	Teacher	Joliet	Illinois
Joe	Evenden	Teacher	Hardeeville	South Carolina
Heidi	Fossum-Anderson	Teacher	Princeton	Illinois
Ashley	Fox	Teacher	Joliet	Illinois
Becky	Gray-Clay	Teacher	Johnston City	Illinois
Patty	Hall	Teacher	Bellevue	Nebraska
Rachel	Halper	Teacher	Northport	Alabama
Nikole	Hample	Teacher	York	Pennsylvania
Jarrod	Hankins	Teacher	Dixon	Kentucky
Maynette	Hardin Stroud	Teacher	Vilonia	Arkansas
Nicole	Harris	Teacher	Joliet	Illinois
Monique	Haug	Teacher	Henry	South Dakota
Brittany	Hurst	Teacher	Corpus Christi	Texas
Jennifer	Ibeling Zindel	Teacher	Washta	Iowa
MaElena	Ingram	Teacher	McAllen	Texas

Mike	Jaissle	Principal	Cleveland	Ohio
Sarah	Janzen	Teacher	Bellevue	Nebraska
Judy	Jennings Queen	Teacher	Joliet	Illinois
Mara	Ki	Teacher	Perth	West Australia
Katie	Kikos	Associate Principal/Athletic Director	Chicago	Illinois
Jackie	Kosik	Teacher	Highland Park	Michigan
Kirsten	Larson	Teacher	Middletown	Illinois
Melissa	Leal Shafer	Teacher	Los Fresnos	Texas
Damian	Lee	Teacher	Essex	England
Amy	Lewis	Teacher	Lewis Center	Ohio
Tami	Little	Teacher	Sergeant Bluff	Iowa
Sue	Luken	Teacher	Waverly-South Shore	South Dakota
Theresa	Lyness	Teacher	Niagara Falls	New York
Jen	Marshall Baker	Teacher	Rochester	New York
Janice	Matheson Klinzing	Teacher	Medina	New York
Kimberly	McMahon	Teacher	York	Pennsylvania
Lisa	Mendler	Teacher	Brooklyn	New York
Sandra	Miller	Teacher	Buchanan	Michigan
Brandi	Morgan	Teacher	San Antonio	Texas
Penny	Moses	Teacher	Perry	New York
Christel	Norwood	Teacher	Joliet	Illinois
Maureen	Notaro	Assistant Principal	Batavia	New York
Christa	Palmer	Teacher	Batavia	New York
Sharon	Pantera	Teacher	Medina	New York
Brianne	Pearson Alexander	Teacher	Manatee County	Florida
Joanna	Phillips-Mock	Director	Mt. Vernon	Georgia

Becky	Powell Rehbeck	Teacher	Hilliard	Ohio
Dave	Raffel	Principal	Germantown Hills	Illinois
Rick	Ransanici	Consultant/Special Education	Dansville	New York
Lori	Rehmert Keller	Teacher	Greenville	Ohio
Jennifer	Rutkas	Teacher	Joliet	Illinois
Jerry	Ryan	Teacher – retired	Rochester	New York
Elisa	Ryszkiewicz Kirby	Teacher	Cheektowaga	New York
Sarah	Salminen	Teacher	Buffalo	New York
Gina	Salvatore	Teacher	Upper Arlington	Ohio
Patti	Sanchez	Teacher	Los Fresnos	Texas
Jessica	Schirrmacher-Smith	Principal	Franklinville	New York
Dave J.	Schmit	Teacher	North Sioux City	South Dakota
Bev	Sklar	Teacher	Joliet	Illinois
Zach	Stein	Teacher	Kewanee	Illinois
Shawnna	Sweet	Teacher	Rochester	New York
Lisa	Thielen	Teacher	Heron Lake	Minnesota
Laura	Tobia	Teacher	West Seneca	New York
Chelsea	Weisensel	Teacher	Joliet	Illinois
Melissa	Wroblewski	ICT	Medina	New York
Sara	Anne	Teacher	Niagara Falls	New York
Tara	Marie	Teacher	Niagara Falls	New York
Adrian	Torrese	Principal	Perth	Western Australia
Kelly	Smith	Principal	Perth	Western Australia
Dr. Wendy	Claussen	Professor of Education, Southwest Minnesota State University	Marshall	Minnesota

TABLE OF
CONTENTS

Chapter One   **Desperate for Attention**   4
Teacher: Amanda Sherman, Students: Jacki
and Juan

Chapter Two   **Oppositional Defiant**   9
Teacher: Jamie Easton, Student: Cole

Chapter Three   **Severe ADHD**   13
Teacher: McKenzie Connelly, Student: Jameson

Chapter Four   **Disruptive, Out of Control**   18
Teacher: Marissa Macko, Student: Darryl

Chapter Five   **Problems Working in Groups / Sarcasm**   23
Teachers: Christa Gribbs, Karen Mosceller
Student: Nicco

Chapter Six   Helping Kids and Teachers Help Each Other   31
Teachers: Bern Smith, Jennifer Sterm, Christine Bobby,
Students: All

Chapter Seven   Dealing with Kids who Leave Class and Have
Trouble Connecting   36
Teachers: Christa Palm, Laura Klimek, Student: Michael

Chapter Eight   Struggling Reader   41
Teachers: Grace Taska, Anthony Coli, Student: Alex

Chapter Nine   Structuring a Successful Special Education
Program   45
Teacher: Charlene Barrett, Student: Cheyenne

Chapter 10   Building Confidence thru Success   49
Teachers: Justin Young, Jennifer Heeley,
Student: Alex Snyder

Chapter 11   Improving Student Attention and Focus on   53
Specific Tasks
Teacher: Lindsey Demerle, Students: Whole Class

Chapter 12   Behavior Charts   58
Teacher: Bob Wentz , Students: Whole Class

Chapter 13   Challenging the Oppositional Defiant Student   61
Teacher: Shana Miledele, Student: Patrick

Chapter 14:   Negotiating with Student   64
Teacher: Millie Jedroo, Students: Whole Class

Chapter 15   Winning Over Your #1 Trouble Maker   67
Teacher: Christina Ramirez, Students: Whole Class

Chapter 16:   Teaching Behaviors You Want to See   69
               Special Education Department Staff
               (High School)

Chapter 17   Fair vs. Equal, Accepting Late Work,
               Rewarding Everyone   75
               Teacher: Shelly Nagle, Students: Whole Class

Chapter 18   Setting Limits   80
               Teacher: Laurie Bushnell, Students: Whole Class

Chapter 19   Mentoring, Reflecting, Working with Parents 82
               Administrator: Cheryl Corey, Assistant Principal,
               K-8 Building

Chapter 20   Diffusing Anger in the Moment   87
               Teacher: Jenna Hall, Student: Frank

Chapter 21   Fun in School!   89
               Teacher: Kaitlyn Jones, Students: Whole Class

Chapter 22   Using Teases to Motivate, Listening to Advice 91
               Teacher: Rebecca Sittel, Students: Whole Class

Chapter 23   Teaching Students Where They Are   97
               Teacher: Theo Trist, Student: Ashley

Chapter 24   Stop Being Boring!   106
               Teacher: Geoff Taylor, Students: Whole Class

Chapter 25   Start with Your Best   109
               Teacher: Colleen Pituala, Students: Whole class

Chapter 26   Maybe you are in the Wrong Profession   111
               Teacher: Kaitlyn Van, Students: Whole Class

Chapter 27   Teaching and Using Manners   113
               Teacher: Feliz Ogbaama, Students: Whole class

Chapter 28   My Special Education Model   115

Introduction

Dan was seated to my left and Mike was directly across from me. I had nine students in this self-contained SPED class. There was an empty desk directly next to Dan. The desks were arranged in a horseshoe with me in my rolling chair at the opening facilitating a discussion on the civil war. This was always one of my favorite topics as it generated heated but engaging discussion. Both kids were known to be volatile. Privately Mike was working on walking away from arguments and fights when he felt angry. He was allowed, without asking, to get up from class and go to the psychologist's office two doors down. Dan did not know Mike was working on this as I am a firm believer in privacy.

As the discussion continued I noticed Dan getting aggravated. Mike was arguing his point and without hesitation quickly picked himself up to leave. Dan, believing Mike was coming toward him, jumped over a desk and punched Mike in the face. I grabbed Dan by the back of his green Nike hooded sweatshirt and pulled as hard as I could. He stumbled backward, turned around, picked me up by my shirt collar and threw me onto my desk. He cocked his fist to punch. Anthony, a six foot three, 200 pound football player ran full speed across the room and tackled Dan yelling, "What are you doing? You can't hit a teacher!!! Are you crazy?!?!" Dan then snapped out of his rage, looked at me and said, "Oh my gosh Mr. Mendler. I am so sorry. I would never try to hurt you. I am so sorry." He crumbled to the floor and sobbed uncontrollably.

Dan was suspended for two weeks. I remember the day he came back. He walked in with his head down. I taught my lesson and he did not say a word. At the end of class he walked up to me and said, "Mr. Mendler. I am so sorry. Sometimes I completely lose control of myself. I am on medication now that will help." I said, "That is great. But if this happens on the street you go to jail. End of story." He said, "I know. I get it. I promise things are going to change. I am truly sorry." We shook hands as we had done many times in the past. I told him to go home. He got almost to the door and stopped. He turned around, looked me directly in the eye and said, "Mr. Mendler. You know you were kind of light, right? I mean, if you want I will stay after school and work out with you!" He ran out.

This was by far the most challenging day of my career. It is never appropriate for a student to put his hands on a teacher. But after every difficult situation I firmly believe in looking in the mirror. What can I do differently to prevent this from happening in the future? I was taught to keep my most challenging student closest to me. So Dan was directly to my left. He was separated from Mike by three students and two empty desks. I prevented Dan from fighting about 10 other times that year. But every time I approached him from the front. This time I yanked his hood from behind and his instincts took over. I should have had Mike next to me and Dan across from me. Now Mike gets up to leave and Dan comes toward me. I get in front of him and probably break it up before a punch is thrown.

After this incident I decided to get really good at classroom management. I studied, researched, and taught the most difficult students in a variety of different schools. I now have the best job in the world. I travel all over the world helping teachers succeed with their most challenging students. I observe classes, listen to problems and do small group or individual consultations with teachers. A secretary takes notes during these consults and from those notes I type a report for each individual educator or group. These reports are written in anecdotal form and contain dozens of practical advice and strategies for educators to use immediately. I do my absolute best to write and say it exactly as I see it. I want to warn you before reading that this is not a traditional book. It is not research based. There are no citations or studies. It is literally just feedback in its purest form. The only things I changed are teacher and student names. I hope you find it helpful. Enjoy.

Chapter One
Desperate for Attention

Teacher: Amanda Sherman, Students: Jackie and Juan

Jackie is obviously the biggest problem I see while I am here at this school. She confronts other students and always has something to say even if a situation does not involve her. It is obvious she loves to be the center of attention. My first suggestion is to allow Jackie to have the last word with you. You say to her, "Jackie, it would be appreciated if you minded your own business." You say this privately. As you walk away she mumbles under her breath. Instead of continuing to walk away you turn and engage her. This is a classic mistake that many of us make. Do not engage. Allow her to mumble. Pretend she says, "Right now I have to call you a couple names under my breath because if I don't I am going to look like a wimp in front of the entire class. Can you please the mature adult and continue walking away from me? I have to eat lunch with them I have to ride the bus with them, I have to be around them all day long. After all Ms. Sherman, what do you tell us to do when someone calls us a name? You tell us to just turn and walk away.

How come you can't? You tell us to just ignore it. How come you can't? And if you did I would really appreciate it thank you very much ma'am." Amanda is concerned how it will look to other students if she lets Jackie mumble. Will they believe it is ok to call her names then too? This is a valid concern. You can eliminate this by using a prevention phrase. Tell your students what is going to happen before it happens. "Guys listen up. Unfortunately (which means I wish this was not going to happen but I know it is) some of you in this classroom this year are going to do and say some rude, nasty, inappropriate mean things. I know you are!" Student: "How do you know Mr. Mendler?" Me: "Good question little 12-year old. It happens every single year of my life. I just want to let you know if and when it happens I will not always be stopping my lesson to deal with it. It does not mean I didn't hear it (because probably I did) and it does not mean I am not going to do anything about it (because there is a very good chance that I will). However, in the actual moment it might look to some of you like I am ignoring a certain behavior. That is how it might look to some of you. But trust me I am not ignoring it. It just means I think teaching is more important in that moment. Is there anything you all do not understand? For example, I might drop by your desk this year and say, 'Knock it off!' As I am walking away you might call me a skinny, tall, ugly, bald ass geek. Your best friend might go, 'oooohhhhhhh, oh, dang Mr. Mendler! You heard that! Oh shoooooot!!!' Like she is giving birth. Trust me, yes I heard it and yes I am going to do something about it. It just might not be in the moment you all think I should. And let's be clear about one more thing. If there is a consequence it will be between that student and me and nobody else. I will not share everyone's business with the entire class. Sound good?" I explain to Amanda that she now has ultimate control. She can stop and engage if she chooses or continue walking away without worrying about what everyone thinks.

It is a constant battle for attention with Jackie. Sometimes she sticks up for the teacher, telling other students to be quiet or do their work. I ask Amanda how specifically she handles it when Jackie does this. Amanda reminds Jackie her job is to be the student. I recommend: Pull Jackie aside and strongly compliment her. "I love when people are assertive and thanks so much for sticking up for me. It means a lot. At the same time do you see how it might look like I do not have control if you are fighting my battles? What do you think about allowing me to correct them next time? If I am unsuccessful you can have a try. Sound good? But I really do appreciate you sticking up for me." Notice how I phrase the important points to Jackie as questions. The real issue is her need to feel and get attention, power and control. I teach Amanda the five basic reasons kids misbehave. Attention, Power, Control, Competence, and belonging. Much more on all of these as we continue.

Jackie often gets in trouble by retaliating against another student who makes her mad. Almost always the retaliator gets caught. Teach Jackie how retaliating hurts her! "You often get in trouble, but I know it is not usually you who starts it. Do you understand how the way you react to other people can get you in trouble? Do you want to allow other people to control you?" She will not think he controls her and probably get defensive. "He doesn't control me!" Response: "Can you see how it seems like he does? If he says X you immediately get really mad. In your mind you are sticking up for yourself, right? This is understandable, but the way I see it he is controlling you. If he tries to make you mad and you get mad he wins." If she sees being tough / in control as not reacting then she will understand the more she is pushed the calmer she becomes. Keep reminding her not to let anyone control her emotions. Every time point out that when she reacts to him she is giving up her power and control.

Juan is obviously desperate for attention as well in this class. Remember to compliment what he does well while ignoring the nonsense. Even some of the annoying things are good qualities. Try giving him as much control as possible. Use questions to get him working for you. "How many questions should be on the test? I was thinking we should play a review game. Want to help me decide which game to play? What do you think about this homework?" Remember, the behavior we see is merely a symptom of something greater. I tell the story of my leaky roof. I was having never ending problems with my roof leaking. The drip was in the kitchen. Because I have zero handyman skills I put a bucket under to catch the water. When the roofer came to fix the problem I noticed he was banging on the complete opposite side of the house. I said to him, "The problem is in the kitchen not over my bedroom." He replied, "No, the kitchen is where you are seeing the problem. But actually the water is getting in over here and travelling all the way down to your kitchen." Often in school the behavior we see in our classroom (the drip) is really coming from somewhere far away (home life is a huge one). Remember, the root cause for almost all behavior problems is a student's desperate need for Attention, Power, Control, Competence, and Belonging. Learn the five causes. Memorize them so whenever a behavior occurs you can see them instead of the drip.

When we view the behavior as just a symptom it allows the teacher to stay calm and focused. Addiction is another good example: Many addicts say they have a drinking or drug problem. In reality alcohol and drugs are not the problem. They are the solution to the problem(s) of abuse, neglect, depression, anxiety, etc... and the person escapes the problem with drugs. Fix the root of the problem and squarely deal with the real issues and the addict can truly heal.

Amanda asks about her learning lab that is 20 minutes long. They don't listen and are not quiet. She does not like to give detention for talking (good!). Detention does not usually fill a person's need for Attention, Power, Control, Competence, and Belonging. Be honest with them. Say, "Obviously what I am trying to do right now is not working! I want to know from you what I can do differently. I can write you up! I can give a consequence. But we all know that does not work. How about everyone gets 10 minutes to talk and then you give me 10 minutes of solid quiet work time?" Remember, negotiating with kids in school is fine! Again notice how I ask questions instead of giving statements.

Amanda asks about a reward system. If you are going to do it my recommendations are: Make the list of sought behaviors as a class. "This is what I was thinking, what do you guys think?" Reward the entire class in honor of a person or group of people. "Because I am so proud of how Juan behaved today everyone gets an extra 15 minutes of talk time tomorrow in honor of him. Great job Juan."

Chapter Two
Oppositional Defiant
Self-Contained (very low functioning)

Teacher: Jamie Easton, Student: Cole

Cole is the one she wants to discuss. Jamie says he was a little better today. He is basically set off any time a teacher expects him to do something he does not want to do. Try hard to avoid minor power struggles over taking off headphones or being quiet. Second to last word is so important with kids like him (see Amanda Sherman for explanation). Focus on using questions instead of statements. Instead of saying, "You need to take off those headphones, or you aren't doing what you are supposed to be doing." Try saying, "What do you need the headphones for? How long do you plan on using them? If you choose not to take them off at the agreed upon time what should the consequence be?" Oppositional / difficult kids will argue just because they can. Questions are much harder to argue than statements.

Jamie asks what to do if he refuses to answer. Just say, "Ok, I guess you are not going to answer so I unfortunately I have to make the decision. But if you change your mind let me know and we can talk about it." Then get out of there. Do not stick around. Remember, 2nd to last word! Think choices and questions in all situations. I ask about Cole's mental capacity. Is he able to have a discussion if it is something he wants to talk about? I am told he talks about technology all day. He loves taking things apart and putting them back together. Jamie needs to do as much of this as possible. Go to garage sales or on the internet and find broken electronics or devices. Allow him to fix them. Show him how he can buy something, fix it and resell it for a lot more money. List the items on Ebay. Allow him to write the description (ELA) and figure out shipping costs (math). You can use Ebay to teach multiple real life skills. Jamie lets me know in the morning Cole is usually pretty well behaved. He is also good when he has a class job (he feels power and control). He recently lost Ipad privileges and is working to earn it back. Jamie is deciding when to give it back. I recommend bringing him into the process. Again, you want to make him feel like he is in charge. Say, "I have an amount of time I think it should be gone but I want to know what you think. How long will it take for you to remember breaking things is unacceptable?" If he says one day you might say two weeks. Negotiate to a week. During the week praise him for making a decision and let him know he is doing well. You might even give it back to him early. Bring him into decisions being made about him. You can always take it further. "So if you get it back in a week but break it again, what should happen then?" Notice how I am continuing to prevent problems by asking questions. Get him to make the same decisions you were already going to make. If I was his teacher there would always be some type of project for him to work on related to taking apart and fixing technology. I might even look to purchase a television for myself that is broken and have him work to fix it. I love that he is so interested in this.

We also discuss the social aspect of other kids knowing he is in that room. Today he said, "I'm really mad at my mom for putting me in this room." I ask how Jamie responded. She said, "Well it is too bad. There is nothing I can do about it." Here is what I think the response should have been. "I understand that you feel upset and I probably would be mad too. I promise I get it and I am really sorry you are in here. Is there anything I can do to make it better? I was not the one who put you here but I can show you how to get out! Acting up when you get the opportunity to go into other rooms does not help. It actually makes the other teachers think this is the right place for you. Even though we both know it is not. I will advocate for you to move out of this room but only if I can count on you not to make yourself look bad by misbehaving when you leave my room."

Jamie understands the home life is a mess. Mom does not usually follow through. No dad, and step-dad cannot stand him. No wonder he is difficult! I recommend taking him and kids like him for a walk (around the school) once in a while to talk about home. If he won't talk about his you talk about yours! Explain things you have struggled with in your life. How have you overcome them? Become an inspiration and a role-model as well as a teacher.

Try helping him find a safe place to "unload" his baggage without getting in trouble. As always I remind Jamie she is not allowed to quit on Cole. He makes you want to give up.

But you are not allowed. View him as a challenge and try hard to see the small gains he has made. It is so easy to focus on the negative. Sometimes we need to take a step back and really look for the good. The technology idea I gave will definitely help a lot.

Jamie asks if she should let go of what happened earlier or if disruptive behavior should "carry over" between periods. Never hold grudges! This is for school and life! It is too short. Always go with what you see in front of you. Otherwise we spend the whole day annoyed (self-contained kids always do something to annoy the teacher)!

I am told Cole has a chart where if he behaves he gets to visit the high school to see vocational programs that might interest him. He should be allowed to visit immediately without a chart. In fact, bring him there yesterday! Help figure out which program best fits him and start finding activities based on that now!

Chapter Three
Severe ADHD

Teacher: McKenzie Connelly, Student: Jameson

Jameson is a name I hear from many teachers throughout the day here. McKenzie tells me he can only focus for so long. Welcome to all kids. Just because the school says a period is 45 minutes does not mean a student can focus that long. Break the period into four ten minute mini lessons if there are kids that lose focus quickly. Take either the first five minutes to talk to them (relationship build) or the last five for questions. Show them the written agenda. For example:

8:50-9a:	*Warm up activity*
9-9:10a:	*Group activity on angles*
9:10-9:20a:	*Walk around the school looking at and measuring angles*
9:20-930a:	*Begin homework / questions*

At the beginning of class McKenzie says, "I'll wait" for class to be ready. This is very dangerous! I rarely say that. Teach hard right from the beginning. Sort of like a bulldozer, just keep plowing through (unless of course they are asking questions that are on topic), otherwise some kids will keep you waiting all day!

McKenzie thinks things have improved since the start of the year. We discuss Jameson. It depends on the day with him. Yesterday was mostly good. He kicked a desk on his way in but other than that remained on task. He even helped other students. I ask if you intensely (and privately) praise him for this. Get right in his ear, "I love how you are helping others. I am so proud of you. Great job! I love it!" Many of us correct kids with extreme intensity. "I said knock it off! Cut it out! Enough is enough! Stop it!" Jameson has learned the way to get attention is to be bad. Then he is noticed. People pay attention to him. This means he must be praised with the same level of intensity. Try hard not to do this in front of other kids! The goal is for him to learn the way to get attention is to do the right thing!

I give my personal insights on ADHD medication. I make clear I am not a doctor but my severe ADHD and tremendous personal success on medication make me a self-proclaimed expert. I explain that rarely do kids say they do not like meds. What they often say is, "I don't like how this makes me feel." Bingo. This means it is probably working. Most take time release medication. One of the major side effects is that it messes with the appetite. For the past 15 years I have taken 54 milligrams of concerta, which is the highest dose you can take (well I guess you can take more but I don't recommend it!). I eat a huge breakfast every day. Breakfast is the key to my day, because like I just mentioned the medication takes away my appetite. Then take my pill. It lasts 3-3.5 hours before beginning to wear off. Yes 3-3.5 hours! Many medical experts will tell you it lasts all day. I am not saying they are wrong. I am saying this is not the case for me. So, let's say I take my medication at 8:30am. Around noon it begins to wear off. I get edgy, moody, easily annoyed, and most importantly, really hungry. Hunger is the critical piece to this. I must eat lunch during this "window." Whether I eat or not, the med kicks back in (time release) after about 45-50 minutes and the window closes. Now I am not hungry anymore. For many kids in school their "window" does not match their lunch. Think about how hard this is for a young person. 20 minutes ago she is in social studies starving. Finally she gets to lunch. Unfortunately the window closes and the med kicks back in. Now the student is not hungry anymore. Almost always she says, "I don't like how it makes me feel." Try to figure out where the "window" is for certain kids. Does it match lunch or PE? Remember, the timing of medication makes a huge difference. Try to match their strongest dose times to big tests or long periods of seat time. "Snack time" is common in elementary classes. Again this is great if the snack time matches the window. Instead just allow kids to eat when they are hungry. The alternative is to teach them about their "window." Good luck with a bunch of seven year olds. It is much easier to encourage eating when hungry. I always have a big bag of apples, bananas, and carrots on the shelf in my room.

Mackenzie is teaching "point of origin." Not bad but definitely add at least one specific example. Maybe use sports? Where does a game start? The point of origin: 0-0. Origin = Original or origination. The game originates (starts) at points 0-0. Pay attention to how many times you say, "for example" in a day. The more the better. My wife is a high school math teacher. I tell how she takes students on a field trip to the gym. She uses lines on the court to teach angles, X & Y axis, etc... Students start at a point of origin (place where two lines meet) and physically plot points with their bodies (3, 5). She shows how angles are all over the world. Look at ceiling corners for 90 degree angles. Floor curves and stairwells are great for teaching angles as well.

Mackenzie seems hesitant about this! I tell of visiting my brother in Columbus. He is a blood cancer specialist. He came home from work with tears in his eyes. I asked what was wrong. His response, "I made a mistake today at work." Me: "Oh. That happens all the time." Him: "And an 8 year old boy died in front of me." Have you ever been in a situation where you have no idea what to say to a person you care about? We sat in silence. About 10 minutes later he looks at me and says, "Sometimes I wish I worked in a profession where I did not always have to be perfect. I mean, when I operate I must be perfect every single time. I never get to make a mistake. It is an incredible amount of pressure. Teaching would be really cool because you are trained professionals that go to work every day with the ability to dramatically impact a life. But the worst thing that happens when you make a mistake is the kid comes back the next day, right? I would love that. I would just experiment all the time." That conversation really hit home because I do not think most of us look at teaching this way. We often see things as life or death when really nothing ever is. Allow yourself to experiment. Make mistakes. Have fun. Admit when you make a mistake and correct it. Great teachers make a ton of mistakes but they do not make them twice.

Ask kids what they think in different situations. I tell about one of my most difficult students, Tara. She constantly made little comments and jokes with two other girls she sat next to. I couldn't get her to stop. One day I kept her after class. I was really frustrated and basically out of anger said, "I don't know what to do with you anymore! If you were me what would you do?!?!?! In a very calm voice she said, "I would just move my seat." I said, "What?!?!?!" She said, "I said I would just move my seat. The problem is I don't have any friends." I said, "What do you mean?" Her: "How many meanings does that have? I don't have any friends. I don't even like the girls I sit near. But I have to laugh at them and act like they are funny. Because when we leave here they sit by me at lunch. They talk to me. They want to be around me. But Mr. Mendler, please do not move my seat like most teachers do it." I had no idea what she meant, but luckily my para-professional did. The rule is at least three for one. If I have to move a seat I move three. This eliminates, "You always pick on me you never pick on anyone else." I actually left Tara alone and moved the other two. Sometimes students give us great ideas. She did not disrupt my class again. My para said, "Maybe you want to ask their opinion more often!"

Chapter Four
Disruptive, Out of Control

Teacher: Marissa Macko, Student: Darryl

Marissa enters our meeting angry! I ask why she is so upset. She tells me, "Administration here does not support us! I have sent Darryl to the office like 40 times this year and they always just send him back. He is so disruptive, difficult and out of control and I am disgusted by the lack of support." I ask, "What would you like them to do?" Marissa: "Um. Well I mean there is just no support. These kids are out of control and nobody seems to care." Me again, "I hear you. And I am asking for your input. What would you like to see done?" Her, "Well I don't really know. All I know is these kids show no respect to anyone...." Blah blah blah. I can't stand when teachers complain that they are, "not being supported." What does that even mean? Supported how? Do you even deserve to be supported? There is nothing worse than a teacher kicking a kid out of class and then complaining that the office is not doing a good enough job. You had your chance and failed. Now you are mad that someone else is failing? This is like batting leadoff in a baseball game and striking out. Then your teammate bats next and strikes out and you get mad at him for not supporting you? Ridiculous. You had your chance first and whiffed. Marissa looks at me like I have three heads but calms down. Stop worrying about being supported and start working at becoming successful with that student!

We talk about Darryl. I ask my basic relationship question. Tell me about his home life? Marissa, "Well it is not good I know that. I mean I can tell you right now it is bad. I believe... I mean I am not 100% sure but I think he has a few brothers and sisters and I know, well I am not sure but I think there is a mom. Wait maybe it is grandma..." I stop her. This time I ask Marissa to ask me about the home life of a student I struggle with. It sounds like this. "It is bad. He has three brothers and two sisters. His mother is a nice lady but completely overwhelmed. She tries hard but works two jobs so supervision is minimal at home. His older siblings are not super interested in helping parent. Three years ago their father walked out on the family. Just picked up and left. Did not tell anyone where he was going. This devastated Darryl and now he does not trust adults. Especially adult men. Deep down he thinks everyone is going to abandon him so he has built a wall around himself. Last year he tried out for basketball but got cut. This was awful not because of basketball but because he desperately needed something to belong to..." A relationship takes time, patience, energy, and effort. There will be setbacks! Marissa has not even begun. This is where she needs to start. Without a relationship there is no chance with Darryl and the cycle will continue.

Once the relationship is built to a point where he trusts a little bit, she can focus on the real reasons he is misbehaving. As always, Attention, Power, Control, Competence and Belonging will play a part. In fact, a fundamental issue at this school and with kids in many places I work is a lack of feeling power and control. This school is filled with teachers giving commands and expecting kids to follow, like they should be obedient puppies following orders. For some, even if they want to comply they will fight because of how statements are phrased here. Once again, I recommend using questions instead of statements. Stop telling and start asking. I explain school is not set up for kids to feel power and control. Many feel power and control somewhere else in their lives so they do not need to get it in school.

I highly recommend focusing on changing one or two students instead of five or six. Go with Darryl because you instinctively mentioned him when first asked about your class. I tell her she needs him more than he needs her. The goal is to become teammates instead of adversaries. Look for as many ways as possible to bring Darryl onto your team. Make him your helper. For example, pull him aside and privately ask, "What should the homework be? Here is what I was thinking of teaching today what do you think? How many questions should be on the quiz? How about you help me write the quiz?" Bring him into the mix as often as possible with as many decisions (let him feel power and control) as possible. Do this with consequences as well. Say, "Well I kicked you out of class seven times already and it is obvious that has not worked because you are behaving exactly the same way. I am telling you to your face I do not know what to do with you. Do you have any suggestions for what might work? Because I do not really care about the consequence I just want you to stop calling people names."

See McKenzie Connolly example of asking student opinion out of pure frustration!

She asks me what you do when they are in the middle of doing something inappropriate. Is that the best time to have this conversation? Yes and no. Questions are almost always better than statements with difficult kids at all times. But prevention is critical too. First thing in the morning when they are walking in get in his ear and say, "Hey what's going on with you? How are things going to be today? What can I expect? Can I count on you to behave? How many minutes of good behavior do you think I will see?" The answer depends on the student and severity of the behavior. Hopefully it is something I can walk away from in the moment (2nd to last word). Notice how my questions are firm, direct and short. This gives the teacher an idea of what is coming. Is this going to be a good day or bad day, a good morning or a bad morning, a good ten minutes or a bad ten minutes? The younger the age the more frequently I check in. Generally it does not work for anyone to be a part of a reward system that requires them to be good all day or all week. Many think, "All day?" I can't be good for 20 minutes, let alone all day. Have quick meetings before lunch with your tough ones. Let them tell you how they believe they are doing. Say, "I have my thoughts but I want to know what you think first." This forces kids to think about being responsible and lets them know right now at nine in the morning that at 11 in the morning I am going to talk to my teacher and have to explain to her how I think I did. This is another form of giving power and control. A classic symptom of an oppositional kid is their never ending need to feel power and control. Generally their home lives are a mess. With many oppositional kids there is very little structure at home. It is a free for all. Kids do whatever they want. Mom is not there or mom is weak, meaning nothing she says is what it means. She says be in at six for dinner and her son walks in at nine. Not only is there no consequence but mom says, "Here is your dinner honey and I will clean it up for you too!" Now this kid comes to school and is a disaster. School is all about limits. Wait in line? I don't wait in line at home! Wait my turn? Raise my hand? Share? This student has never learned how to do these things.

I notice you say the words "I need" a lot. Eliminate these words. If kids cared what you needed they would already be doing it! Replace "I need" with: Thank you for... I would appreciate if... What do you think about? Do you mind? It would be great to see... I can only imagine coming home from a work trip and saying to my wife, "I need you to do my laundry! I said cook my dinner! Where is it? Did you not hear me correctly?" I know this sounds basic but always remember to talk to kids the same way you would talk to anyone else in your life.

Chapter Five
Problems Working in Groups / Sarcasm

Teachers: Christa Gribbs, Karen Mosceller, Student: Nicco

Nicco is obviously a handful. But I actually think he is pretty funny. He shouts out often in class. My immediate suggestion is to give him a specific number of times he is allowed to shout out. Or you can let him choose the number and then monitor it. The goal is for him to track his own behavior (give him a sense of power and control). Remember, if a student is running full speed (metaphorically) we must get him to slow down first. The goal is to reduce the number while getting him to think about his behavior at the same time. This is true as well when you call on him. Say, "Ok Nicco it is your turn and you get one minute to answer (or however long you want to give him)." Kids like him need specific start and end times or they will ramble on and on! The lab area is a main concern of Christa's. It is hard to give directions and get them to listen. My suggestion is to move quicker and give directions before they move to that area. Obviously safety comes first, but moving quicker forces students to get right to work. Think about how long an activity should take. Tell students they get half that amount of time. The goal is to create a sense of urgency. Most will get right to work. Then the teachers can focus on the slower groups / partners. You ask me about group work / cooperative learning. You tell me, "It seems like any time I leave them alone to do an activity there are problems." I watch your activity and it is pretty clear there is basically zero organization to the group work. Here are my suggestions. I use English because it is primarily what I taught. Obviously you can modify for whatever you teach.

- **Groups should have no more than five members.** Four is ideal, but I can live with five. Six or more is a recipe for group disaster.
- **Each member must have a specific role to complete**. I suggest numbering each member of the group one to five. Then each is given a task. Numbers one and five will stay the same no matter what content or grade level you teach. Two, three and four will change based on the activity. Role number one is the group leader. It is amazing how many teachers I work with that do not have a group leader in every group. This is the most important person. The teacher is the General Manager of the team. Your name is on the door. Group leaders are like the managers on the field, making sure everyone else on the team is successfully doing their job. Number twos are the readers. Threes are note takers. Fours are note organizers. Number fives are presenters. Five cannot do her job without four organizing notes. Four can't organize notes if three is not taking them. Three can't take them if two is reading too fast or too slow. And number one watches to be sure all

are doing their jobs. Of course, create any categories that fit your specific needs or lesson.

- **Change up roles**? Not always. The Yankees do not put their starting shortstop at catcher just to "change it up." Try putting students in positions where they are best. Some are natural leaders. Others are better at reading. This is not the time for me to teach a student how to read. The only role I require is "presenter." This is because students rarely practice public speaking in school.
- **Give specific instructions:** Once groups are seated and quiet we can give specific instructions for each member. I like to make it the group leader's responsibility to help get his or her group focused and paying attention. Group leaders need to write down the instructions for all members. Each member only writes down his specific role.
- **It is always easier to extend than it is to take away**. Figure out how much time the activity is going to take. Then cut it in half. For example, if I believe an activity will take 10 minutes, I tell students they have five. By giving less time we create a sense of urgency, and there is a greater likelihood they will get right to work. If students are working well and five minutes pass I can extend another few minutes without anyone knowing. By contrast, try taking time away, and someone always complains.
- **Bring groups back but allow slower groups to finish**: It is common to hear someone say, "But we aren't finished yet." It is important that we extend the time if most groups are not finished. However, if it is just one or two allow them to finish while beginning the next thing with everyone else. This way the

finished groups are not bored while waiting for slower groups.

- **Red Cup - Yellow Cup - Green Cup.** Give each group leader a red, yellow, and green plastic cup. If the leader concludes that the group needs help that will take more than a quick explanation, he puts the red cup in front. Yellow means the group has a quick question that needs a quick answer. When green is visible, it means all is okay. This allows us to avoid being the annoying teacher that constantly asks students if everything is ok. It also gives the teacher a few minutes of chill time.

- **Only talk to the leader:** Say this to the class: Hey class, just so you know, during group time there are only six people in this room that are allowed to talk to me. If you are not a group leader I do not want to hear from you. You go to your group leader. If they can't help they will come to me." Now instead of managing 30 students, we only have to pay attention to six leaders. Like captains on a football or soccer team who take charge on the field, group leaders allow us to manage a large group while focusing and dealing with only a few. This is how we get students working for us.

I recommend you stop worrying about noise level if kids are on task unless it is completely out of control. Obviously students are louder in a lab environment. Close your door!

I like that Christa is really in charge of her class. She stands tall and gives clear, concise direction. Sometimes she is a little bit sarcastic. Just be aware and do not be afraid to apologize if a student does not get your sarcasm. Use words like please and thank you more often when giving direction.

Replace the words "I need" with "I would appreciate" or "Thank you for." Sarcasm to me is an interesting tool. Many educational experts recommend never be sarcastic with kids. I do not agree with them. I almost never use the words *always* or *never* in education. To me sarcasm is like an extremely dangerous chemical in the chemistry lab. If you do not know how to use it stay the heck away because it will blow up your relationship with a student. But used properly it can often be a strong relationship building tool. My rules for sarcasm are:

1. **When using sarcasm you are joking about something**. If the student does not get the joke apologize quickly and passionately. "I am so sorry. Sometimes I mess around with people. I was totally joking with you. I made a mistake. It will not happen again."

2. **If you are able to dish it you better be able to take it!** I worked with a teacher that used sarcasm with kids and when they retaliated she wrote them up. No way! A student got me good one time. One of my high school seniors had a brand new bright yellow polo shirt on. He was African American. The shirt looked really good on him. I said, "Chris! That is a great shirt I love it. It looks really good on you. Of course you know it would better on me, right? Because I look better than you and there is nothing you can do about it. So keep working on your looks." The class laughed. Chris looked at me and said, "Yeah good one Mr. Mendler. But you know what I do have on that would look fantastic on you?" I said, "What?" He said, "Hair bitch!" The class erupted. I got mad. That is how I know he got me good. We smiled, laughed, shook hands, and moved on. Some people will tell me never to do that? I do not agree with them! Be careful and use it sparingly. Christa and Karen are having minor issues with the warm-up activity and class right after lunch. Many hate writing and it is hard

to get them to self-start. I recommend showing an example of what you want. Even if you did an example yesterday or earlier. Do not assume they remember, because usually they do not!

I also recommend grading everything. Tell them that you are grading how they come in and sit down. "Everything counts" is a phrase I often use in my classroom. Give some easy quizzes to get students feeling good about being there. Say, "All you have to do is come in, sit down and do the warm up and you get a 100% quiz grade. How easy is that?" Never tell kids something doesn't count. Everything always counts in my room. How you say good morning, how you say please and thank you, how you fail a quiz counts. How a student fails helps me determine if I should allow them to retake it. Do they fail quietly or do they blame everyone else and distract the class?

We discuss Kiha for a bit. She often influences the class in a disruptive way. After lunch is a difficult time. I recommend giving the loudest person the job of quieting everyone else down. Both agree this might work with Kiha because she is a leader, though often in a negative way. I recommend using this to your advantage and viewing it as a positive. Get her to work for you instead of against you. Pick out leaders and work hard to get on the same page as them. They will often influence everyone else! I also say it is ok for a co-teacher to leave with a student(s) who looks like they need some help / time away from the class.

Make sure to look for patterns with kids. Is it the same time / scenario every day? What is going on at home? What you see in class is almost always a symptom of something greater. I give the "runny nose" example (see Mr. Trist / Ashley).

Did you ever consider the warm-up as a group activity? Each day a different group is in charge of creating and teaching the warm-up to the entire class. I tell the story of Jessup Winters, one of my former students. I was in the middle of a lesson that was going really badly. From across the room he yelled, "Yo Mr. Mendler, you have no idea what you are doing right now do you?" This was the most on-task statement he had made all year! I replied, "Actually no. Can you teach it better?" He said, "Well I certainly could not be worse!" I threw him the whiteboard marker and he started teaching... He was good. So I sat down and started disrupting class like he normally did. He completely ignored and kept teaching. In fact, he walked over, got right in my ear and said, "Knock it off Mr. Mendler," and then he walked away! He is not supposed to know how to do that! After about 10 minutes I stopped disrupting. I didn't mean to stop but I was not getting to him. Jessup literally taught 43 minutes straight. I kept him after class and said, "I do not like being embarrassed in front of the class. But you do have a career ahead of you in education if you choose." He said, "I know." And he walked out. Teaching ability yes social skills not so much!

I explain if there is a catalyst that makes a student worse, do not do that thing (giving Nicco detention for late / homework). Sometimes in education we learn what to do by figuring out what does not work first. Can you find ways to help him get homework done in school? Does he have a free period or time during the day?

Do not ever forget the fundamental responsibility of a teacher is to make the lives of kids better. If something is making it worse, stop doing it. I know this sounds really simple but at the end of the day it is true!

Chapter Six
Helping Kids and Teachers Help Each Other

Teachers: Bern Smith, Jennifer Sterm, Christine Bobby, Students: All

Bern asks what type of advice they should give teachers to help understand where these kids come from (home lives, etc...). She says sometimes the most important thing in a child's life is not always school. Amen. I explain that I thought about becoming a social worker or counselor but my parents would not help me pay for it because social workers are often caught in the middle between kids and teachers, like the net in a ping pong match. It is a tough job. When helping adults (other teachers) show how your advice is in their best interest. Many teachers are not interested in student home life or building relationships. They are interested in content. Help them see the relationship building process as an investment. Use the analogy putting money away now so it is worth more in the future.

I teach them to focus on working with the student instead of the teacher. All of the counselor questions to this point revolve around helping the teacher. Switch your focus. My question to the student when he complains about a teacher. "Do you want to be successful in her class?" If the answer is "no" I say, "Ok, would you like to have her next year?" If the student says they don't care, etc... I say, "Ok good luck." I am willing to give 100% effort all the time but the student has to meet me part way. If they want to learn how to succeed in that class I teach the following:

1. You are not allowed to speak in her class. Talking gets you in trouble. You are now only allowed to speak when she calls on you. Even then I recommend being as short and sweet as possible.

2. Say "good morning," to the teacher on Monday and Friday. Students that say good morning to their teacher regularly get a ½ grade higher than kids who do not. Do not stick around for a conversation. Say good morning and sit down right away.

3. If a student hates a teacher with or without reason, my question to the student is, "Do you want to make a lot of money in your life?" If they say yes I ask, "Who is your favorite actor / actress?" Student: "Denzel Washington." Me: "Did you see Remember the Titans? He was an amazing football coach. In real life he never coached football. But we believed he did in the movie. He pretended to be something he never was." The goal for the student is to pretend to be something or someone that he is not. Actors do not make huge money unless they are good. "Your first role is to pretend you like the teacher that you hate. Remember I am not asking you to like her. I am asking you to pretend you do!" Then focus on this every day.

Let students blow off steam in the counseling office. All of us need a safe place where we will not be judged. Explain how getting frustrated and angry actually gives the teacher what she wants. "Every time you lose control the teacher wins. If you hold your temper, you are in control and you win." I like to use the words win, lose, and control. "Do you want to win in her room? Every time you call her a name you lose control of yourself. She wins and you lose. Do not let her beat you!"

At a staff meeting all counselors, psychologists, social workers, and support people stand up and explain your strengths to teachers. Many of us do not know how to utilize you. Give occasional updates about kids. I realize you cannot be specific. For example, "Hey everyone, Bobby is going through some really tough things at home. Please be extra compassionate this week. If you work with him directly please come see me so I can fill you in a bit more." Communicate often and clearly with teachers.

I explain how my self-contained students often want to go to the counselor instead of staying in class. I recommend bringing counselors in, instead of sending kids out. One of the best things I ever did was have my counselor teach a lesson every Friday afternoon on a social issue kids were dealing with. I tell them about a counselor I used to work with named Dana. I often sent kids to her instead of the office (the goal for them to return to class). About two weeks into this she came to my room and explained the kids were getting in trouble on purpose so they can see her. She suggests flipping it on them. Most students do not have counseling built into their schedule so they are not sure when and if they will ever get a chance to meet with Dana. Dana asks if she can come to my room once per week to teach a 20-25 minute lesson on a different social skill / topic. For example, her first lesson is on drugs and alcohol. The kids who disrupt my class during the week have to go with me to her office during this time. We end up doing this for the entire year. It is amazing. Just knowing they are going to see Dana calms many during the week. It also gives me a break from the monotonous content. It allows us to dive head first into some serious issues the kids are dealing with. I am a big believer in bringing counselors and administrators into the room instead of sending kids to them. Have them come during class time to help with an individual student or to be a part of teaching the content.

I believe that switching classes is good for kids. They will have bosses in life they do not like. Different personalities, styles, and rules are good. Teach kids that they cannot control the teacher, but they have control over how they act. I constantly preach to control the only two things they have control over. *Attitude and effort*. Outcomes in life take care of themselves. But attitude and effort can always be controlled in every situation.

Jennifer asks how you get teachers to buy in (sort of the same question). My response: "It is not easy. That is what I just spent the above section explaining. The focus has to be on kids instead of teachers. Teach kids to change and teachers will follow. This is not the normal type of thinking that many bring into the day. But I promise it is the right place to spend your energy." I also make clear that it is ok for kids to fail sometimes. Failure is a part of life. If you choose to do nothing then you fail. Failing because a student gives zero effort is different from failing because the work is too hard.

The counselors keep asking me about changing teachers. The good thing is it is easy to see that they are focusing on the wrong thing. Focus on kids! Kids are usually easier to change than teachers! Another counselor talks about taking kids to a professional hockey game and how it is viewed by many other teachers as a reward for bad behavior. I rarely respond to other teachers who complain about what I am doing. Teachers report to administrators, not other teachers. Who cares what other teachers think! Everything does not need to be explained or justified to everyone.

I tell them about my School Psychologist friend, Mr. Kilgore. We had a secret system. If a student entered his office from my room holding the book *A Lesson Before Dying* it meant I needed a 15 minute break. I was not mad. I do not want him written up or in trouble. I just need a break. I also had a bright orange pass in my room that meant strangulation thoughts were entering my mind. This pass meant he needed to hold the student longer!

Chapter Seven
Dealing with Kids who Leave Class and Have Trouble Connecting

Teachers: Christa Palm, Laura Klimek, Student: Michael

Today's lesson was a review of multiplication and division. Christa and Laura are co-teachers but not together all day. Christa teaches Math and Science all day. Kids switch to another teacher for ELA and Social Studies the other half. The SPED teacher follows the kids. I prefer the SPED teacher follows content. Michael is their most difficult student. He was not here most of the class because he went to the bathroom. He was gone 15 minutes. He was supposed to be gone two minutes. This is often a problem. The aide was at lunch, so Christa could not send her to look for him. At the beginning of the year he was gone three times a day for 20-30 minutes. So this is actually an improvement. This behavior is not just in this class but others as well. He has a sheet / chart to keep track of goals set by counselors. He had some input creating the chart (which is good). I believe kids should always be a part of creating their behavior plan or IEP. After all, it is their plan! Michael is given the sheet at the beginning of every day and at the end of each class the teacher gives comments and points based on how well they think he did. If he does not present the sheet then there are no comments or points given.

My recommendation – Let him rate and grade his own behavior. Then he compares his grade / rating to the teacher grade for him. They mutually agree on what he deserves. This is how to truly teach responsibility. Remind when he leaves class to keep track of his points. Have him say how long he will be out when leaving for the bathroom. You can even ask him for a consequence suggestion if he is not back on time. Say, "I know this will not happen because you can be trusted... but if you are not back in five minutes what should I do?" Again, the goal is getting him to take some responsibility for himself. Instead of being annoyed that he took too long be upset that he didn't keep his word on the amount of time he is gone. Say, "Michael, I am really upset because I thought you were able to make decisions for yourself. Is this not true? You said five minutes and it has been 10. Are you not a trustworthy person?" Notice how I am not emphasizing him being gone for too long. My issue is him not being able to make decisions and keep his word.

I teach them a strategy called "Take a shot." Students get the opportunity to tell the teacher why he / she is wrong about something in two minutes or less. If uncomfortable speaking they can write it. I tell the story of when I was teaching 4th grade. I saw a student kick another student. It happened right in front of me. I decided she was not allowed to go on the field trip. Her take a shot went like this. "Ok Mr. Mendler. I admit I kicked her. I did it and I shouldn't have. That's what you call taking responsibility, right? But here is the thing. I was going to kick her about nine other times and I didn't. Isn't that what you call self-control? In baseball if I was up 10 times and I got nine hits would it be really good or would I be in trouble? Because I feel like I was nine for 10." If I allowed her to go is not the point (I bet you want to know!). It is always interesting to see each situation through student eyes.

We talk more about Michael's sheet. I believe the number of behaviors is overwhelming. There are literally like 50 items for him to improve. Stay in your seat, bring a pen, do not disturb others, raise your hand... just to name a few. Many are broad and subjective. "Be respectful" is on the sheet. I explain that respect means different things to different people. Respect is a value not a rule. A value tells a student *why* and a rule explains *what*. For example, the value is *respect*. The rule is hands and feet to yourself. Notice how the rule is specific and measureable. This is evident in our society. The rule when driving is specific. 65mph. Seatbelts buckled. 66 is speeding. It cannot be argued. The rule does not say, "Be respectful of other drivers." This of course is impossible to enforce.

With Michael, try to predict and preempt by using questions instead of statements. "I am thinking about checking the camera, if you were hitting another student what should I do? Should there be a consequence? If you were me what would you do because I am at a total loss? If there were two things I could do to make this class better for you what would they be?" I ask Christa to choose a day and from the time she wakes up until the time she goes to sleep she can only ask questions to everyone in her life. Example: "Ms.

Palm, what is the homework?" "Great question. What do you think the homework should be?" "How many minutes do you think you can focus at a time? How about eight on task and then eight looking out the window? Can you keep track of how many minutes or should I? I am sure you won't but if you do disturb others can we agree on a consequence right now?" Part of being a teacher is being in charge. Part of being in charge is telling people what to do. This does not usually work with kids like Michael. My prediction is this becomes the way you teach. Questions force students to look internally and often get them to make the same decisions we would make for them anyway.

Back to the sheet: I recommend you and Michael pick one or two tasks to work on. Once complete cross them off. Ask him if there is something you can work on as well. Try to make it a team approach.

We discuss the difference between success in school and success in life. I believe they are totally different. To be successful in school a student must be really good in many different areas. Math, Science, ELA, Foreign Language, Phys Ed, Music, Art, etc.. In real life that same person has to be outstanding at one thing. When is the last time you boarded a plane and said to the pilot, "Before we take off can you please explain four causes of World War II?" No. Get me up and get me down and do it in the right place. I do not really care what else you know how to do. Ask students to think about what their one thing will be in life!

Do not be afraid to praise Michael just for showing up. For some students life is easier when distant and guarded. They are afraid to get close to adults because of a deep fear of being hurt. This is often the root of the problem. Tell him what the problem is and that you totally understand it.

Example: "You have moved nine times and been in six different schools. I am guessing you are not very interested in getting close to adults because you don't trust us. And you know what? I would be exactly the same way. I really would. In fact, I think it is incredible that you come to school. It isn't right you have moved so much. But just so you know, I am not going anywhere. Even if you move again I will check on you. I will follow up. I will be here. Once a person gets into my life it is really hard for them to get out. So get used to me!" Notice the passion and energy I say this with. Michael might tell you this is not true. Just say, "Ok. But if you ever do want to talk about it I am here." Then move on. Get out of there. As always, this is done as privately as possible.

Another suggestion is for Michael to keep a personal mini notebook. At the end of each day, or class (or hour or 15 minutes) he gets to write one positive statement about himself. The teacher can add to this if she wants. We conclude by discussing the difference between a problem that a teacher sees and a symptom of the problem. I tell her my leaky roof story (see Amanda Sherman). I explain that the symptom is *going to bathroom, touching others, defiance, etc...* But the real problem is almost always Attention, Power / Control, and Competence / Belonging. For him it is probably abandonment and a combo of the above five. Focus on the foundation of the problem (cause) rather than the symptom and usually you will see change

Chapter Eight
Struggling Reader

Teachers: Grace Taska, Anthony Coli , Student: Alex

Grace does most of the content teaching. Anthony does most of the modifying and explaining. Do not worry that you have different roles. This is inclusion. As long as both people understand and are comfortable with their roles it is fine, especially for the first year together. By the second year Anthony will do more content teaching as he will have gone through the material once. Grace tells me Alex Snyder does not volunteer unless he knows the answer for sure. Grace watches closely for him to volunteer and calls on him when he does. His reading is at 3rd grade level and he is definitely a problem in other rooms.

Grace does not like to know ahead if kids are a problem. This is because they are not usually a problem for her, even if difficult for others. My opinion is that she has the personality where failure / mistakes are ok in her room. She is completely comfortable modifying content based on student ability. Grace asks if there is anything else she can do with struggling readers. I recommend relentlessly getting in the student's ear. Say, "You are ok. I see lots of improvement. Mistakes are not a big deal." Tell the student that struggling with reading is not that big of a deal (even though it is). I tell her the story of a high school teacher that once told me, "Just so you know Brian, reading is overrated. You have to know how to do it. You do not have to be amazing at it." This was the complete opposite message I was used to. Telling me this took the pressure off. By not caring so much I did better. Anxiety always affects performance in some way.

I tell Grace I often misbehaved before having to do something that was uncomfortable or difficult. Any time you want a student to read out loud (in front of the class) give the passage the night before. Then that student goes first. This way he prepares and gets it out of the way as soon as class starts. Once finished the student can listen and pay attention to others without worrying about which passage he will read. Grace tries to get participation without making kids feel uncomfortable. I recommend nothing should be random. Even when the teacher says, "I am randomly calling on someone…" It should not really be random. Cold calling should be rigged. Do not create an environment where a student can look bad in front of the class. A rule to remember: In general, Sped kids do not like surprises.

Grace is always thinking about how to make kids feel comfortable in class. I tell her that generally kids are not the problem. Think about it. If 1st period has no problem and 2nd period has a problem the only difference is the teacher. Energy from Grace keeps kids from being bored, along with her obvious love of content.

She struggles to involve Anthony as a co-teacher. Again, I tell her not to worry about this. Both teachers have roles. Remember, the SPED teacher is still learning content. They will not be able to teach it as well as the Gen Ed teacher. We discuss homework. Grace tries not to assign too much and is very aware that many of these kids come from difficult home lives. She realizes that homework is not the most important thing for many. If a student is not going to do homework he needs to find the teacher and tell her why it is not done and when it will be complete. If you do not find the teacher, then you fail. There is nothing wrong with failing kids unless the teacher is literally giving them work that they cannot do.

Grace also seems a bit worried about burn out. She works a lot of hours trying to be a perfectionist. I recommend trying to compartmentalize your life. Plan lessons that "bleed" into the next day. Show more of the movie in class. Seeing the movie takes out the step of visualization while reading. We discuss the difference between movies (have time limit) and books (no time limit). When reading something that is not in the movie, stop and discuss. Should this be in the movie, and what do you take out?

Try hard to stay mentally strong. Do not let pressures from what you are supposed to do (from administration and the state) get in the way of doing what is best for kids. Learn to give up some control. Sometimes the best way to stay in control in life is to give up some control.

Use the four question teacher evaluation. Get students ready as though they are taking a regular test. At the last second say, "You know what... I am proud of how hard you have worked this week. Instead we are doing a four question quiz." Questions one and two are, "What are two best things about me as a teacher?" Questions three and four, "What are two things you do not like about me as a teacher?" My rule for this quiz is they cannot get in trouble no matter what they answer. "But Mr. Mendler, we love you there is nothing we would change." Me: "Ok then I guess you will get a 50% on the quiz." "But Mr. Mendler we hate you!" Me: "Ok then I guess you will get a 50%. Because I believe that no matter how much you love someone there are always two things they can improve on. No matter how much you hate someone there are always two things you can find that you like." I have no problem with teachers playing games in class. However, be sure students do not look bad in front of each other. Give some students the question and answer the day before (same concept we discussed with struggling readers). This is the question you ask them publicly during the game. Again, the goal is always to get students feeling good about your class.

Chapter Nine
Structuring a Successful Special Education Program

Teacher: Charlene Barrett, Student: Cheyenne

Char mentions how hard it is when Cheyenne does not take her medication. Sometimes we have to do the best we can where we are in the situation we are in. Remember effort and attitude are the only two things anyone can control. Attendance is pretty good except for Cheyenne. Char understands Cheyenne very well. The mom reads at a 4th grade level and is not interested in Cheyenne becoming successful. Char explains that the baggage often comes out as attitude (which she often sees from her mother). Cheyenne is not afraid of anyone or anything.

Homework is generally a problem because her parents can't do it. So obviously it rarely gets done. I say stop giving it! Instead just do the work in class. This is self-contained! No more homework. Do everything in class all the time. Once in a while give homework to the one or two who might actually do it. Use the fact you are not giving homework as leverage with students during the day. Say, "C'mon guys. Give me another 25 minutes of hard work. You know I'm not requiring very much at home. This will change if you do not give me energy and effort during the day!"

Char likes that she can do her own thing but struggles teaching all content areas. Of course she does. I do not like the structure of self-contained the way it is done here. Middle and High School Self-contained kids should switch classes like all other kids. I always say if we took the 10 best kids in the school and put them in one room with one teacher all day within two weeks they would become disturbed. And we do this with our worst!

I recommend Char get as many lessons as possible from General Education content teachers. She does this as often as possible but admits she could do more. Then modify Gen Ed content to fit your kids. Gen Ed teachers should be writing some type of lesson plan. Copy it as best you can. If teaching all content areas is too overwhelming (which it probably will be) pick the two you are best at. Focus on those and sprinkle in a bit of the others within those lessons. Char went to a workshop on how to use common core with SPED students. It did not offer much help. In order to teach them content we need to know what their interests are. The goal is to bring our content into their world instead of forcing them into ours.

Try not thinking too much about students not being able to get or understand content. Certainly do not let it discourage you! This is self-contained. They often do not get things. Just keep teaching and pushing as hard as you can. Focus on building relationships, getting to know your students, and teaching social skills. Teach please and thank you, good morning, eye contact, how to shake a hand, and job interviewing skills. Do not be afraid to show movies related to content. The whole thing! If there is time left you can read the book. Most teachers do the opposite.

Char tries to make it as fun as she can. Students are really into the play that they wrote. She found out one of the kids is a really good actor and is hilarious. These are skills / qualities to now embrace and encourage. Maybe he can join the school play or musical. Many of these kids just need something to belong to. Push him to get involved by literally walking him to the auditions. This can become his reason for coming to school.

Try the same type of method to get students interested in math. Char tells me that same kid loves getting in front of the class to do math, but hates doing it on paper. He probably loves the attention he gets from the class. He is a good actor, funny, and likes getting in front of people. Work at feeding him a healthy dose of attention every day as often as possible. Get right in his ear and let him know what an amazing job he is doing on basic things. "I love how you walked in this classroom today! Great job walking in! I love it! You walk in on time every day in all classes and good things will happen for you!" Notice the passion and energy that I praise with. As mentioned earlier, we are fantastic at correcting with a ton of energy. "I said knock it off! Sit down! Cut it out! Did you not hear me?!?!?!" This means we must praise with the same level of passion. The need driving the behavior is attention. Be relentless with this. The hard part is ignoring inappropriate behavior. This must be done so he learns the way to get attention is to do the right thing. Many kids have learned the way to get people to notice them is to be inappropriate. Shower him when even the smallest positive thing happens. Ignore when it doesn't. Use him as a leader to help influence others.   This will fill his need for attention.

Char says when kids are off meds it is really hard. Often near the end of the month meds are gone because parents sell them for drug money. Again, these are times to use more videos. Talk to them about how it feels not have their medicine. Do they feel different? Do they talk to you about their parents selling it? How does this make them feel? Talk about yourself to them! Remember, it is all about relationships in this world. Relationships mean I learn about my students and they learn about me!

Chapter 10
Building Confidence
thru Success

Teachers: Justin Young, Jennifer Heeley, Student: Alex Snyder

Jennifer asks about Alex Snyder. He is quiet for the most part. Not defiant, not disruptive and not rude. He just flies under the radar. Jennifer's problem is that Alex does not want to admit she exists. He goes to the aide or Justin but will not talk to Jennifer. She thinks avoiding might be a control issue. In this case I disagree. My guess is it is a Special Education issue. He probably wants no part of anyone thinking he is a Sped kid. Jennifer is clearly the Sped teacher in the room. The more Jennifer tries the more Alex pushes away. If she checks on what he is doing Alex shuts down. For now Jennifer is leaving him alone and Alex is getting work done. I recommend continue to leave him alone... in class.

Find him outside of class. Catch him in hall where there is no Sped stigma. Jennifer has tried but Alex acts the same. Even if it is just the two of them! I say if Alex is not bothering others and he gets work done, just continue to leave him alone. Jennifer asks if Alex is disrespectful by ignoring her. No! Who cares anyway? Remember, the goal is to get kids to learn and do their work. Everything else is secondary! If others question why Alex is left alone tell them they do not need to worry about him. Say, "If you want me to leave you alone, do your work." If Alex stops doing work then adjust. A benefit of inclusion is there is more than one adult in the class so kids have a choice of who to talk to and work with.

Justin asks about positive reinforcement (rewards). I believe if you give rewards many kids will start expecting them. I also strongly believe in rewarding the entire class in honor of a student or a group of students. Justin rewards randomly. I am better with this but still do not love. Be sure you always do it privately. Do not reward one person in front of the entire class. There is a very good chance this will annoy others.

Remember that success and confidence together are a beautiful combination for all people, but especially kids that struggle. The two words breed each other. Think of a clock but instead of numbers the word "success" replaces the 12. The word "confidence" replaces the six. In life confidence breeds success which breeds more confidence which breeds more success which then breeds confidence. Sometimes we have to shove a student into the cycle by feeding them something easy! There is a reason little kids start by playing T-ball. We put the ball on a tee because we understand how important success is. Then we pitch underhand where the coach literally tries to hit the bat with the ball. Why? Because in life success breeds confidence. Then it is overhand pitch. Eventually the child says, "Coach, throw harder. I know I can hit it!" Some of our students have never experienced either.

They ask my opinion of kids who do nothing. I make clear that some kids, no matter what we do are going to say I don't care and do nothing. Let them do nothing if not disturbing others. Nothing in my room is better than nothing somewhere else in my building if I see those as my only two options. Eventually they will hopefully pay attention to something that interests them. I am not saying I want a student to do nothing. But sometimes there is no other option. I remind both of them the bottom line only two things they can control. Attitude and effort. Come hard every day with a positive attitude and give 100% effort. Do not ever quit on a kid.

I let my feelings known about the way SPED is structured here (only from what I have seen). I do not agree with it but within the system teachers are doing the best they can. Justin will do 90% of the content teaching because Jennifer pushes in to multiple content areas each day. Justin is the Science expert. Jennifer is the kid expert. As long as the adults get along, trust each other, and know each other's roles, this will be fine. I much prefer a model where sped teachers follow content instead of following kids. This is explained in detail at the very end of the book.

I explain that inclusion usually fails because of adults. Sometimes there is a resentment between the Gen Ed and SPED teacher. I have not seen this here, which is good. Justin and Jennifer occasionally trade roles. This is fine as long as each realizes their primary role. I explain it is really hard to tell if an inclusion pairing works for three years. The first year the sped teacher learns content. By the second year they are a little better. The third year the sped teacher is now much more of a content expert and can really do much more teaching.

Jennifer likes teaching all subjects because she gets to know the kids better. This is the only benefit of doing sped this way. The quality of instruction decreases though because none of the sped teachers become content experts (most are doing multiple subjects a day).

Chapter Eleven
Improving Student Attention and Focus on Specific Tasks

Teacher: Lindsey Demerle, Students: Whole Class

Lindsey definitely has a rough class. The fact that it is last period does not help. She is aware that Julius loves attention and hates Spanish. A bad combo. I immediately jump in. "Ok then that is your job. Your only focus with him every day is getting him to like Spanish. Every activity, every assignment, how you talk to him, how you look at him... all focused on liking Spanish. Think of when you fell in love with Spanish. What made you love it? What made you decide you want to teach it? This is what you get back to every day all day with him." I tell Lindsey about the "travelling to Mexico" activity my co-teacher used when I taught inclusion Spanish. First she picked a student and asked, "Do you want to travel alone or with a friend?" They always picked a friend. The travelers were then given a scavenger hunt as though they were traveling to Mexico.

Each member of the class not traveling had a role. One was the pilot, another was a flight attendant, and there was a taxi driver once in Mexico to take them to the hotel. But before that their luggage was lost and the baggage person only understood Spanish. Every once in a while a wild card person got to join the trip. Wild card meant the person was allowed to join the trip to help the travelers. They would ask to travel every day! Again, our goal was simply to get them liking Spanish first.

Lindsey tries to make connections with kids but many do not seem to care. I tell her to keep trying. Again, it is never ok to quit on a student or a group of students. I ask how much time she spends outside of class building relationships with the kids in this class. None. This stuff does not happen by osmosis. It takes work! Go out and find them when not required to be with you. This can be done in lunch, during free periods, before school, hallways, and after school. I occasionally will ask another academic teacher if I can have the student for a few minutes during their class time. Many do not mind! Building anything in life requires effort! I believe Lindsey needs to work harder and invest more. I promise it will be worth it. Lindsey admits she needs to do a better job preparing for a tough group at end of day.

I recommend using questions instead of statements. Say, "How many questions are you getting done? By what time will they be done? If they aren't done, what should I do?" I tell her with defiant kids, the more statements you make the more arguing you get. Instead, rephrase everything as a question. "Should I let you go to the bathroom? Last time you were gone for 20 minutes so can I trust you because right now I am not so sure? What should happen if you are not back?" Once again I recommend trying a day of just questions. From the time you wake up until the time you go to sleep all you are allowed to use are questions no matter what anyone says to you. My prediction is this will become the way you teach.

Lindsey tells me about a 2nd period student that says. "Your mama" all the time, swears at kids, and writes on other papers. She is like this in other classes. She does not have many friends. Sometimes she gives attitude to Lindsey. Some days are great and others she will not try. This is normal for not just kids but adults too. Have you ever tried changing something about yourself? Were you totally successful the first time you tried? Probably not. Usually it takes time to change and this is when we are adults and already motivated! Most kids I work worth could care less about changing anything! Try to figure out which need (attention, power, control, competence, belonging) she is most lacking. Remember, name calling, cussing, and disrupting others are all symptoms of the real problem. Yank the behavior out at the root.

The other recommendation is to find out what happened between days. Say, "Yesterday you were great. Today is a disaster. What happened in your life to cause this? I am not mad I just want to try and help you through whatever the problem is. Most importantly, how can we make tomorrow much more like yesterday? Any ideas?" Push her to respond. If she gives you nothing say what you think the problem is. "I am guessing something happened at home. Was your mom drinking last night again? You can tell me. I am not a judge and I am not a police officer. I am a teacher." Tough kids are out on a limb. Sometimes we need to go out there to get them. Remember all of this is done as privately as you possibly can. Finally, do not be afraid to tell them personal things about you. Really get to know them. Focus more on kids and less on content! Remember the things that can always be controlled. Effort and attitude. Give your all and keep a positive attitude and I promise good things will happen.

Lindsey believes Jaquan lacks confidence. Many in the group are really good friends and feed off each other. Lindsey tells me, "Every other day they forget the procedures." My response: "Give your class a real quiz that counts the second they walk in on the procedures. For some this will be the easiest quiz they have ever taken."

When I observe the students are recording people's ages. Topic is numbers. Kids are wandering around the room counting items. Sort of like a scavenger hunt. It is disorganized. Lindsey calls it "planned chaos." I do not believe it is that chaotic. Disorganized yes, chaotic no. Be sure in the future when you do any group activity there is a specific end time (see Christa Gibbs / Karen Mosceller page 23). Then constantly give cues for how much time they have left. If you are not sure how long an activity should take do your best estimate. Then cut it in half.

I tell the story of when I taught in a 9th grade Spanish class. We had 42 students, many of whom were in Spanish 1 for the 2nd or 3rd time. One was Pablo Ramirez. SPANISH WAS HIS NATIVE LANGUAGE! He spoke it better than the teacher, but literally did nothing. I was sent in to help with behavior since I spoke zero Spanish. The first thing I noticed was many walked in late. As kids were entering my co-teacher had 10 Spanish words on the board with their English translations. She did this every day. On Friday she gave a quiz on all 50 words. It was a disaster. Horrible grades, nobody cared, etc... My recommendation: Monday morning the words are on the board for the first five minutes of class. On Tuesday there is an open book open note quiz on Monday's words right after Tuesday's words are given (first five minutes of class). Wednesday open book open note quiz on Monday and Tuesday's words. Same thing Thursday. Then on Friday a closed book closed note quiz on all words of the week. Immediately Friday quiz grades went way up. Just from the sheer repetition of writing the words correctly every day during the week. This is with no more homework or studying! Just writing the words over and over again correctly made many successful. If you do it as a real quiz grade not only are they learning, but their overall grades increase. During the closed note quiz on Friday many students now have something to lose. Plus there are lots of quizzes so if you didn't do well, there is another tomorrow. As time went by Thursday's were closed book as well. This was powerful for improving grades and getting them to class on time!

Chapter Twelve
Behavior Charts

Teacher: Bob Wentz, Students: Whole Class

I notice a behavior chart on your wall. Each student name is across the top of the chart on a cut out airplane. Across the bottom are three categories for behavior. Smooth ride, turbulence, and crash. He asks what I think of the system. My answer, "Who cares what I think. In fact, who cares what anyone thinks. The only thing that matters is does it work and is it effective?" Out of 31 students on his wall 27 of them are smooth, three are turbulent and one crashed. He tells me, "Yeah 27 of them are good all the time. They are never the problem." My answer, "Then why do you have a chart for them? You just told me they are always good. That's like giving 27 people wheelchairs when they can walk perfectly fine on their own!" He asks me, "Ok well then what do I do?" First get the chart off your wall. Individual behavior is not a decoration for your classroom. On one hand we tell kids non-stop all day to mind their own business. Then we put a behavior chart on the wall for all to see. We do not get it both ways. Either we want them to mind their own business or we don't. Now that it is off the wall for 27 of them we do nothing. Because they can walk perfectly fine. You said it yourself. They are always smooth. Now we look at the remaining four. Three are turbulent and one crashed. I ask him to tell me about each of the four. The first is constantly getting out of his seat. Literally cannot sit still. Up down up down all day. So he gets a chart that is between him and the teacher and nobody else and it focuses on one thing and one thing only. Sitting still in his seat. If he is up 15 times a day the goal is to get it to 10. The chart goes inside his desk. He is now smooth, turbulent or crashed but only based on one thing. Let him tell you where he believes he belongs instead of you telling him. At first it is every half hour. Then we move to every hour, etc... The goal is for him to take responsibility for his own behavior.   Do the same with each student that is turbulent or crashed. Now instead of a generic chart on the wall for everyone that is public, embarrassing, and fixes no one, we have individual charts for individual kids based on individual things they struggle with.

Mr. Wentz has an incredibly loud and booming voice. There are times he means to talk privately to a student, but the whole class can hear because his voice carries so much. We agree this should be focused on. Do not be afraid to pull kids out of the room to talk to them privately. I do not generally recommend this but with him it might be helpful.

I notice a little girl volunteers an answer and is incorrect. You say, "Nope. Anyone else want to try?" I am not sure you notice the look on her face. Her eyes shoot down and her smile turns to a frown. What an awful way to respond to a student that just took a risk. How about, "Great guess and I can totally see why you think that. In fact, probably many others in the room see it like you do. Unfortunately that is not correct, but awesome guess. Thanks for taking a chance." I continue to reiterate it is our job to make kids feel good! This does not always mean they will succeed. Our job is not always to make them succeed. This is not possible. Failure is a part of life. Making someone feel good while failing is an incredible skill that is rarely worked on but makes a huge impact on classroom management.

Praise praise praise. It is so easy to forget to praise kids. The more we praise the more we can criticize. One does not work without the other. If I am always criticizing and correcting then I become predictable. Here comes Mr. Mendler again, always telling me what I did wrong. I send my message and the student's guard goes up. My message bounces off. At my workshops teachers often tell me, "I don't get what the problem is. I mean I have told him the same thing 50 times so far this year. When is he going to learn?" I respond, "That is your problem. Every once in a while mix your message up and catch the student off guard. Walk over and say, I love that shirt where did you get it?" Be sure to praise kids for doing the right thing even if it is what they should be doing. Remember, praise (and correct) as privately as possibly.

Stay organized. Organization might be the single most important quality as a classroom teacher. My suggestion for this is simple. Find the most organized teacher in your building and do exactly the same thing they do. Once the systems are in place you can adjust based on your own style. I'd like to see a written agenda on the board so kids and the teacher know exact times things will happen during the day. This has been shown multiple times already.

Chapter Thirteen
Challenging the Oppositional Defiant Student

Teacher: Shana Miledele, Student: Patrick

We talk about Patrick. He is driving her nuts (her word not mine!). She admits maybe being a bit too hard on him. He is labeled Oppositional Defiant and Shana has no idea what to do with him. He argues everything constantly! I explain to her where oppositional defiance usually comes from. Almost always it is traced back to a kid that gets so much attention at home they have no idea how to live without it. Sometimes mom is even afraid of this child. They run the show. There is only one strategy that I know works extremely well with this student. It is called Challenge. I warn Shana, as I do every other teacher I explain this to; it does not sound nice. In fact it goes against much of what we are taught in teacher school and much of what I believe. Always encourage kids, always pump them up, and tell them how great they are. I agree with all of that with most kids most of the time. But oppositional kids are not most kids. With them this generally does not work. So we have to do the opposite. Think about oppositional defiance for a minute. Their nature is to argue everything we do and say. So our approach has to change. Instead of encouraging Patrick to do his homework or sit in his seat quietly, I am going to say this. "I know for a fact you will not have all 10 problems done by tomorrow. I guess I will see won't I?" Because he is oppositional he must prove me wrong. In order to prove me wrong the problems must get done. The goal is always to give myself the advantage in the classroom. Saying this puts me in a no lose situation. If his problems are not done (very possible) I say, "See I knew you would not have them done. I know you better than you know yourself." Remember, oppositional kids hate this more than anything. However, there is a very good chance they will be done. If they are I say, "Great. But honestly, anyone can do their work one time. I know for a fact you will not do it for an entire week! I guess I will see won't I?" I know for a fact you cannot sit still for 20 straight minutes I guess I will see won't I? I know for a fact you cannot get everyone quiet after lunch I guess I will see won't I? When I was teaching school and traveling for workshops I would say to my class, "listen I am going out of town for a few days and I expect you to behave when I am gone." Then I let most of them leave. As they are leaving I pull the two leaders aside and say, "except for you guys. Did you hear what I said to the whole class? I lied. I don't care how the whole class behaves. There are only two names on the sub report I am looking for when I get back yours and yours. You see everyone knows you guys can influence the class to disrupt when I am gone but I do not think you have the ability to get everyone to be good. We all know you are leaders and can lead in a negative way but I am sure you cannot lead in a positive way. I guess we will see won't we?" If nothing else I put myself in a no lose situation. If they behave when I am gone I got what I want. If they don't they prove me right which oppositional kids hate more than anything. CAUTION!!! It is critical that what you are challenging the student to do they really can do. I am saying I do not think they can do it but I know they can. If I challenge a blind person to read the board all I do is piss them off even more. This is why so many reward systems teachers use are a colossal failure. The student wants the reward but what they must do to achieve it is impossible. I remember in elementary school if we were good all week we attended "Fun Friday." Good all week? I was not able to be good for half a day let alone a whole week! I recently had a pipe burst at my house and my plumber came over to fix it. We were outside talking when he opened the back of his van. He literally had 100 different tools. He saw me looking and said, "Yeah, I have 100 tools but I really only use the same four or five." This is like challenge. It is a tool you must have in your van but not one that you will use often.

Focus on success. Shana tells me her class is much improved from the beginning of the year. Focus on this and be proud of it. If your school does not have it, create your own classroom on-a-roll. For kids that are improving. Pick up the pace. I advise her to move quicker through her lesson even if every single student is not paying attention. By waiting for the few stragglers you risk losing the rest of the class. Know who the slower ones are and after explaining to the whole class, individually help them. I am told that when observed the recommendation is usually to wait for every person to be completely ready. Obviously I have said multiple times I do not agree. Shana is very easy to talk to and I really like her style. It is obvious she cares a lot about her job and her students.

Chapter Fourteen
Negotiating with Students

Teacher: Millie Jedroo, Students: Whole Class

We talk about the computer and what to do if students will not get off. Remember, kids are predictable. Know what they are going to do before they do it and be prepared! First set a clearly defined limit (15 minutes on the computer). Give warnings as the time gets closer to the end. Be willing to pull the plug if the student does not get off. This might mean they lose work that is not saved. If you give warnings and they choose not to listen the consequence is natural. Then tell the student what he is going to do before he does it! "After 15 minutes if you are not off I am going to pull the plug. You are probably going to scream and call me names and flip out. When that does not work you are probably going to try and make me feel guilty by saying I don't like you, etc... You might want to save all of it and just get off the computer so we don't have to get into it." If he is oppositional this is a great strategy as he has to prove the teacher wrong. To prove her wrong he will get off the computer and not carry on because she told him he would not. He might even get off early! I also recommend questions instead of statements. Get kids to make the same decisions you were going to make anyway. How many minutes do you think should be allowed on the computer? If you choose not to get off in that amount of time what would you recommend I do? Can I trust that you are able to make decisions and stick to them?

Do not be afraid to negotiate! Millie tells me she specifically learned not to negotiate with kids. Ugh I totally disagree. Negotiating is a huge part of what I do. The key of course is to know that students will negotiate then factor it in. If I think 15 minutes on the computer is reasonable I say, "Ok you get 10 minutes on the computer." When he complains that is not nearly enough time I say, "Fine, how many minutes do you think you should get?" If he says, "20" I say, "Fine. I want 10 and you want 20, I will live with 15 but only because I am the nicest teacher you have ever had in your life!"

Use the strategy called, "Take a Shot." This one I invented a few years ago for my students that are going to be lawyers or salesmen. See Christa Palm write-up for details.

Don't ever forget, 2nd to last word is almost always best. Let your students have the last word. There is a power struggle that could have been completely avoided. Remember, tell your kids the first day of school, "Some of you this year in the classroom are going to do and say rude, nasty, inappropriate mean things. I know you are because it happens every single year of my life. I just want to let you know that if and when it happens I will not always be stopping my lesson to deal with it. It doesn't mean I didn't hear it and it doesn't mean I am not going to do anything about it. It just means I think teaching is more important in that moment. Is there anything you do not understand?" Remember, your last word as the teacher is the word, "Thanks." Then get out of there!

Chapter Fifteen
Winning Over Your #1 Trouble Maker

Teacher: Christina Ramirez, Students: Whole Class

C hristina begins by telling me her entire class is out of control. She is frazzled and flustered having just come from 7th period, her most difficult. One of my most fundamental rules has been broken. It is not ok to allow students to get you this upset. And if you do allow it you absolutely 100% cannot show it!

After helping Christina see the first person she must work on is herself, we discuss the kids. I never believe an entire class is out of control. It often looks that way but all groups have leaders. We need to figure out who they are and how to reach them. They usually are able to influence and control everyone else. I use my famous fill in the blank question with Christina. "When X is absent I can get everyone else to behave. Ok fine, X and Y." Christina says, "No it is X, Y and Z." But then immediately says, "But actually when X and Y are gone Z isn't that bad. I think X is really the one." Bingo.

Ok. Think about what we just did with one question.
Instead of "an entire class that is completely out of control"
you have one or maybe two. Mentally it is much easier to
change one or two than 33. These are the two you will
focus on. Remember, they already control everyone else.
Your job is to get them. I would give them as many
opportunities as possible to be in charge in my room. Let
them tell you what the test is going to look like. Have them
get everyone else quiet. Ask their opinion before doing an
activity. The goal is to make them feel important and
successful.

Christina is so focused on computers and content that she
forgets there are real troubled kids in front of her. She
agrees lessons should be put on hold once in a while in
order to really work with kids. I give numerous specifics for
how to do this. Talk to them about their lives. Tell them
about yours. What things do you struggle with? How have
you overcome them? Ask them questions about family,
friends, and relationships. Help guide them through
problems at home with suggestions and advice. Remember
why you went into this profession in the first place.

Chapter Sixteen
Teaching Behaviors You Want to See

Special Education Department Staff (High School)

We discuss a wide range of topics including: behavior plans, rule enforcement, self-contained students switching classes, inclusion, and consistency. It is fine to have a behavior plan for individual kids if it is needed. I do not think a teacher should have one just because other teachers do. I explain not only is it ok for different teachers to have different rules and consequences, but it is actually beneficial. This is the real world. A couple years ago I was working in Nevada. I went to eat at a sports bar the night before my workshop and a man started smoking a cigarette three seats from me. I looked at the bar tender like what are you going to do about this? She looked at me like I had the problem. Oh yeah, in Nevada you can smoke inside (apparently second hand smoke is not an issue here). The reality is Nevada does not change their laws because Brian is visiting. I have to make the adjustment. I believe the best schools are run like the United States of America was originally designed: Individual classrooms and teachers treated like individual states. For the most part each creates its own rules, policies, and guidelines. The federal government (Central Administration) creates policies and rules directly pertaining to safety. Other than that individual teachers get to make decisions and policies as they see fit for their classroom. Obviously the main office offers input and suggestions and keeps a closer eye on the "states" really struggling.

The topic of headphones comes up and across the board the teachers tell me they do not understand why kids are not allowed to wear them. I agree and explain many examples of students using headphones to learn. Since headphones do not usually pertain to safety they should be an individual "state" issue. In a self-contained classroom it is important teachers have every possible tool at their disposal. This does not mean they have to allow headphones. It just means individual teachers get to make the call depending on the circumstances in that room at that time (see above paragraph).

I spend a good amount of time explaining how to teach behaviors you want to see. A teacher says that students often come to her room when they are not technically in her class. She says she immediately sends them back. I agree to a point. However, it is important to teach that student how to behave in the class they are sent from. It is the student's job to adjust to the "state" they are in at that time. However, many need help doing so.

Student: I F-ing hate that lady! She's the worst teacher ever. I can't stand her. Teacher: You are entitled to your opinion and I hear you are upset. I have one question for you. Do you want to have her again next year? If the student continues to complain the teacher continues repeating the question, "Do you want to have her again next year?" Student: "Yes," or "I don't care." Teacher: "ok." Then I can't help you. The student needs to show some type of effort here. It is impossible for me to help a person who is completely unwilling to give any energy toward being successful. However, if the student says, "No, I don't want her again next year," the teacher teaches and then practices the specific behaviors to help the student succeed in that room (Cheryl Corey / Ricky consult on page 82).

The message should not just be, "You are not supposed to be in my room right now so you have to leave." Once the appropriate behaviors have been taught and practiced it is reasonable for teachers to enforce a student being where she is supposed to be at all times.

I am glad this school has departmentalized their SPED staff as best they possibly can. However, you are now starting to see the downsides of departmentalization. Transitions are very difficult for many of the self-contained kids because they are used to being in one room with one teacher all day. I ask the staff to participate in an activity with me. Close your eyes and think about something specific you are really good at in your life. It can be anything but it has to be specific. For example, you can't just say, sports. You have to say, golfing or making lasagna, or painting portraits. Now think about the first time you ever did this. Were you really good the first time? How about the second time? Third, fourth or fifth time and I bet you still were not really good. How did you get better? Getting good at anything starts with first becoming comfortable in that environment. Once comfortable it takes practice, patience, guidance, teaching and more practice. In school we often do the opposite. We "contain" kids that are not good at walking in the hall. The only place to get good at golf is on the golf course. The only place to get good at cooking lasagna is in the kitchen. The only place to get good at walking in the hallway is in the hallway. Remember predictability is so important. Knowing what is going to happen before it happens. Of course transitions are going to be difficult at first. The more kids struggle the more practice we need to do on the skill they struggle with.

Many complain about kids not getting to class on time. First, explain why it is important and how your room will work once students are there. Then give a quiz grade for being on time: There on time and ready to work equals an "A." And yes it really counts as a real grade. I don't generally believe in incentivizing with stuff, but if I value something and it promotes learning and / or better behavior I grade it. See Lindsey Demerle example.

Begin your lesson immediately, even if all students are not present. I am not sure why so many teachers wait for everyone to sit quietly and pay attention before beginning. These same people seem to always be waiting! Be in charge of your room. This means starting when it is time to start. This also means some might not be ready. They will catch up. I strongly believe that ELA and Social Studies teachers should almost always read a book / literature that has a movie. Do not be afraid to show the entire movie first. If there is time left you can read the whole book. Have a specific detailed agenda on the board broken down by times. For example:

8a-8:15a:	*Read and discuss 1 poem and 1 current events article*
8:15a-8:30a:	*Watch Video: Of Mice and Men*
8:30a-8:45a:	*Read what we watched*
8:45a-9a:	*Practice Critical Lens Essay*

When class is ending give a quick explanation of where you plan to start the next day. Of course everything is subject to change depending on student issues and teachable moments.

Constantly correct and praise kids as often, privately, and intensely as possible. Use P.E.P. Privacy, Eye contact, Proximity. Say what you need to say and move. Get out of there. "I love that shirt it looks great on you keep wearing that color!" Or, "knock it off enough is enough stop!" Both done as quickly and privately as possible. Then move. In my room we call it a hit and run. I recently taught this at a workshop and a lady in the back yelled, "I can't move physically." Before I could respond a lady in front yelled, "Then move mentally." The one in the back; "How do you do that?" The one in front; "I don't know. Go ask half the people that are married in this country! Don't tell me you can't be one place physically and another mentally! I have done it for 25 straight years!" This of course was met with a roar of laughter. Fridays around noon most of us start going to another place mentally. Same with Sunday nights. The mental aspect of teaching is almost as important as the physical.

The topic of medication comes up. I do not believe it is ok for teachers to tell kids they should be on medication. However, I believe it is perfectly appropriate (and recommended) to tell kids and their parents all about you.

Obviously I wrote about my own medication use earlier so for me it is true. Others might have to make up a story. For example, "You know Johnny, I have to say that you remind me a lot of myself when I was your age. Smart, funny, but really impulsive. Fortunately I went on this medication... It has literally changed my life. Now I can be funny, outgoing, spontaneous, and impulsive. But I also can be patient, calm, and thoughtful. It is really the best of both worlds. Let me know if you have any more questions about the medication I take and how it continues to dramatically help me in my life." Notice how I make it all about me. The conversation is basically the same with Johnny's parents. The hope is Johnny (or his parents) will ask more questions about his life. If at some point, Johnny seems interested in exploring whether medication might help the teacher can suggest calling or meeting with his parent(s). Remember, you are never suggesting a student takes medication. You are simply being open and honest about how the medication you take helps your life. It makes me so mad when parents refuse to put their kid on medication because "medication these days is overprescribed in our society. I mean when I was in school not everyone was on medication and we turned out perfectly fine." When this happens my response is, "If your kid could not see the board would you get him glasses? Or would you say, 'I don't know it seems like glasses are overprescribed in our society these days. I mean when I was in school not everyone wore glasses. But now it is just glasses all the time!' No. If your kid couldn't see the board most would get glasses. Metaphorically speaking your kid is really struggling to see the board."

Chapter Seventeen
Fair vs. Equal, Accepting Late Work, Rewarding Everyone

Teacher: Shelly Nagle, Students: Whole Class

P retend for a second you are in first grade and I am your teacher. I say to the class, "Hey everyone, I just want to let you know I am so proud of Jennifer. Her behavior has been amazing this week. Because her behavior has been so great she gets two free nights of homework." Are you happy for her? Possibly. But probably you are a bit annoyed because you are always good. She behaves for one week and gets rewarded for it? If you want to get students really annoyed at each other say this. "Jennifer has been amazing this week. She has worked really hard on her behavior. Because she has been so good Jennifer gets to pick any two friends she wants for an extra 15 minutes on the playground! Hurry Jenny we don't have all day." Jenny picks two people and everyone else is annoyed with her because she didn't pick them. Why would we choose to put her in this position? The fix is quite simple. Instead of just rewarding Jenny, reward the entire class in honor of her. "Because I am so proud of Jenny and she has behaved so well this week every single one of you gets an extra 15 minutes on the playground in honor of her. Do not even consider thanking me because I had nothing to do with it. In fact if it were up to me there are a few of you that still would not be allowed to participate. But because of Jenny everyone means everyone. Thank her not me!" Then privately when nobody else is around hand Jenny a free homework pass (if you want). I will argue that she probably does not need it because she now feels so good about everyone getting rewarded in honor of her. Do not make a big scene; do not have an assembly to announce it. Just quickly and privately acknowledge it if you must.

Really understand and implement the difference between "fair" and "equal." Fair means students get what they need. Equal means everyone gets the same. Be fair. Do not worry about treating students all exactly the same way. Say, "I promise you all that I will do my absolute best to be fair to each and every one of you in this classroom this year. This means I guarantee right now I will not always be treating you all exactly the same way. One of you might get 10 problems for homework and another might get five. One of you might get one consequence and another something different for the same exact behavior." Explain this to parents as well. "I will always do my best to be fair to each and every one of your children. However, I will not always be treating them all exactly the same way. One might get 10 problems and another might get five..." It is so important to be as upfront and honest as you possibly can about how things are going to work. This is a huge step in preventing problem behaviors.

During my observation of your class you tell them to "mind their own business" three times. Yet you have a behavior chart on the wall, you ask them to switch papers to correct a spelling test, and you say, "When you are all sitting like Chris it will be time to go to lunch." But you want them to mind their own business?

I am not a big fan of taking recess away from kids for poor behavior. This generally hurts the teacher as much as the student. Most kids I work with will take recess whether you give it or not. Try finding another time for them to do their work. Exercise is important to all of us!

If something is not working change it immediately. Do not wait. Shelly asks me about kids handing in work late. What do I think of this? Should she take it? This reminds me of my first year teaching. I was teaching 7th grade inclusion. I was the SPED teacher and Jim Decam was the Gen Ed teacher. In the middle of March a boy named Anthony walks up to me and says, "Mr. Mendler, here is my summer reading assignment." Please understand this paper was due the first week of September. Anthony is now handing it to me six months late. I smiled and said, "You are kidding right? You think you can just hand a paper in six months late? No chance. Out." Anthony groaned and began walking out. Mr. Decam from across the room, "Anthony, hold on a second. Mr. Mendler here is in his first year. He obviously has no clue how to take a late paper. This time hand it to me so I can show him how." I said to myself, "Oh Shit." This man never missed a teachable moment with kids or adults. I hated him at the time. Today I love him. Anthony walks up and says, "Mr. Decam here is my summer reading assignment." Mr. Decam (shaking Anthony's hand), "Great job man. Not just a good job. Great job. I know writing is really hard for you and I know you really struggle with it. And here is something I want you to remember for the rest of your life. When it comes to anything at all related to education late is always better than not at all. It is always better to come to class late than it is not to come at all. It is always better to hand an assignment in late than it is not to hand it in at all and it is always better to graduate from high school late than it is not to graduate at all. However, late is never as good as on time. And are you kidding me Anthony? six months? Let me ask you a question. Is your paper good?" Anthony, "Yes it is pretty good." Mr. Decam, "Did you cheat?" Anthony, "Obviously I didn't cheat. If I was going to cheat I would have cheated six months ago!" Mr. Decam, "Ok. Let's pretend for a second that you were the teacher and a student handed this paper to you the day it was due. What grade would you give it?" Anthony, "It is good but not perfect. Probably a 92." Mr. Decam, "Ok, Now take into consideration it is six months late, what grade would you give it then?" Anthony looks up, looks down, looks at me, and finally looks at Mr. Decam, "If I was a cool teacher or an asshole teacher?" Mr. Decam (now getting visibly agitated), "I don't care you pick." Anthony, "I pick cool. I would probably do six points a month times six months. That is 36 points off. Plus the eight because it is not perfect so I would give it a 56. But you guys a 56 is way better for my average than a zero right?" Mr. Decam smiled at me. From the first day of school he preached to the kids, "You guys listen to me... Do not get a zero. Zeros will kill you in school. 30's will not kill you. Get a 24! Do something! Write part of the essay. Do a couple of test questions. You can recover from a 30. A zero is almost impossible to recover from!" Mr. Decam believes if a teacher ever looks a kid in the eye and says they are not taking the work they should be fired on the spot. The fundamental thing we do as teachers is take student work and make them better. If you are refusing to do that why are you here? I am not saying I go that far, but my lesson is learned. I always take their work. My policy on late work is that I do not have a policy. I will decide what the grade is in each individual circumstance as the reason the work is late might be different with different kids. I tell this story because Shelly asked me about changing something not working. My point: I am always willing to change to something better the second I learn it. Do not hesitate. Do not wait. Tell students the truth. "Guys I know I said my policy on late work was minus five points per day. But I changed my mind. I will always take your work. Obviously I prefer it to be on time. If it is late I will decide what your grade is at that time. As always whatever is decided will be between the individual student and me and nobody else! Sorry for the confusion." Reward kids with feelings instead of things. Feelings last. Things get lost, stolen, and broken. Make them feel good in your room. When they do not succeed make sure your room is a place that failure is welcomed. Create an environment where effort and attitude are the two most important things. Everything else takes care of itself.

Chapter Eighteen
Setting Limits
Teacher: Laurie Bushnell, Students: Whole Class

Instead of having a sticker chart on the wall for all to see each gets their own individual chart in their desk or at home. It is amazing to me how the same thing continues to be an issue. Privacy is most important. This means sticker charts off the wall! Stickers should be given privately at the end of the day if they are given at all. Of course, the year I taught 4th grade I started my "Sticker Detox Program." "But last year we got stickers Mr. Mendler! How come we are not getting them this year? I want stickkkkkeerrrsss!." The detox program is simple. It sounds like this. "Ok guys listen up. Many of you have been complaining about not getting stickers. But here is the thing. You are all in 4th grade right now, which makes you double digits (10). You no longer want to admit that stickers are cool. They are for little kids like 3rd graders and you are in 4th. So I suggest you start acting like it." Of course if I was teaching 3rd grade stickers would have been for little kids like 2nd graders...

Always think / set up a system from the perspective of your most challenging student. All the other kids will adjust. The most challenging can make life miserable for everyone else. So think like that one or two. How will they feel? Make that your starting point. Laurie has a boy that constantly needs her attention. He basically attaches himself to her. On one hand she wants to help him but on the other he is always distracting her from everyone else. We discuss the root cause of the behavior problem. Laurie understands he is desperate for attention. He basically gets none at home. I am glad she knows clinging is not the problem. It is the symptom of the problem. So how can we give attention without him clinging? I suggest constant choices within clearly defined limits. For example, "Billy, you get to sit right next to me three times today (three is the clearly defined limit). We will be on the carpet six times total. Please pick whichever three times you prefer (choice within the limit)." "We will be lining up today five times. You get to be line leader twice. Which two do you prefer?" By providing the choice after the limit I take the student focus off the limit. Most difficult kids do not like firm limits. So start with the limit but immediately provide some choice. A few other examples of this... There are 20 problems on the page. 10 need to be done for homework (limit). Please pick whichever you think are the easiest (choice). Tomorrow is a test all of you will be taking (limit). There will be 40 questions total and I would like you to pick whichever 25 you prefer (choice). I am guessing the clinginess also stems from some type of home issue. Try to figure out what is going on. Ask him questions and then ask follow up questions.

Chapter Nineteen
Mentoring, Reflecting, Working with Parents

Administrator: Cheryl Corey, Assistant Principal, K-8 Building

I recommend forming a behavior committee. It is made up of student representatives from each grade that you meet with every week. They help set policies, rules, consequences, etc... for the school. Right now everything is done to the kids. They rarely have a say in anything here! This is why so many are desperate to feel power and control. Committee members should include two or three of the most challenging kids in the school from each grade level. Almost like a student council for disruptive kids. Demand that teachers do a much better job building relationships with kids and then hold them accountable. Time for this should be built into their day. The focus is so strongly on test scores and teaching content, that faculty does not see and understand the direct correlation between strong relationships and higher test scores. The teachers know they should have strong relationships with students, but do not really know how to go about forming these connections. Teach them how! The best administrators are not afraid to teach teachers! Explain what we are doing well and what we struggle with. Quiz teachers about their difficult students: (i.e. three interests outside of school, specifics about home lives). Demand that they spend actual class time talking to kids about life, etc... You can bring in the best consultants in the world, or any "behavior program" you want. None is going to be effective unless the kids start feeling like teachers genuinely enjoy being around them and WANT them in their class.

Start a mentoring program where kids mentor kids. Try to have your most difficult older students mentor your most difficult younger. This would be awesome for Ricky. Ricky's home life was as bad as I have ever seen. Physical, sexual and mental abuse.   But Ms. Stillwell was amazing with him in second grade. This year he is really struggling in 3rd grade because the teacher is not nearly as good. I recommend Ricky go back to 2nd grade to be Ms. Stillwell's class helper at least a few times per week. He loves her. She built such a strong relationship with him last year and he will be great in her room helping students just like he was. Ms. Stillwell is all for it and tells me she really misses him. This also gives Ms. Beavers, his 3rd grade teacher, a much needed break a few times per week. I truly believe this will be as big a help for Ricky as it is for the kid he mentors. You can have 6th graders work with 1st graders, etc... Again, as a school you must believe this is important and understand focusing on this will bring higher test scores. Heck, they can't get worse! Mentoring is powerful and I do not see much of it going on.

I believe there is not enough time set aside for "bullying prevention and intervention." Kids here need to practice what to do instead of bullying. For example, Ricky was sent to the office because he hit a student who said something about his mom. He was very clearly able to articulate to both Cheryl and me exactly what happened. "I know I am not supposed to hit, but I got mad. I am supposed to walk away and tell her I don't care what she says. And honestly, I really don't care what she says, but I cannot really help it." He then told us next time someone does or says something like that he will respond by walking away etc... In most schools it ends here (or Ricky is given a consequence). But I told Ricky we were now going to practice to see if he was truly able to do what he said. I told him to pretend I was a student. I then said, "Ricky, your mom is soooooo ugggggggly!" Instinctively he cocked his fist as if to hit me. This was DIRECTLY after he just finished saying he would not hit. I stopped him and said, "Ok, no good. We have to try again. Ricky, your mom is sooooooo ugggggglyyy!" Same response. He cocked his fist as if to hit. Long story short.... It took us nine times. Yes, nine practice sessions before he actually said, "I don't care what you think about my mom," and then walked away. Bottom line is that district level administration should build time into the day for kids like Ricky to actually practice and role play these scenarios. Practice is usually the key to success in life.

You have a "reflection room" where kids talk about what they did wrong, write on a piece of paper what they will do next time, and miss recess. This is a decent start, but definitely not enough with the population you are working with. The same few are here every day. The teacher in the reflection room can take it to the next level by practicing and role-playing different scenarios with kids, like I did with Ricky. But you need to teach that person how to do it. I also believe the teacher needs to write down what he did wrong, what he will do next time, and sit with the student during recess. Remember any time there is an argument or power struggle at least two people are involved. The teacher must take responsibility for his part in the problem. We discuss block scheduling vs. periods. If done properly I am a big proponent of blocks. I like 80-90 minute blocks where kids are seen every other day for an entire year. This is beneficial for a number of reasons. First, it keeps them out of the hallways half as many times during the day. Each changing time is then longer. So you might have an 80 minute block with six to eight minutes between classes. Clearly enough time to go to a locker, get a drink, go to the bathroom, hug your girlfriend and still get to class on time. Transitions and disruption generally go together. Naturally fewer transitions equal less problems in the hall. Second, teachers only teach a particular class two or three times in a week (T,TH or M,W,F). Much better if you do not get along well with a given student. Teachers must learn how to teach in a block. It is critical that they break up the content into different categories so students do not get bored.

8:00-8:20: Poems / Bell Ringer / Current events
8:20-8:40: Read "Of Mice and Men"
8:40-9:00: Watch Video "Of Mice and Men"
9:00-9:15: Discussion / Begin Homework / Questions

Even within a period teachers should have a structured agenda. This helps kids and teachers stay focused. It also helps the teacher organize what exactly they are going to teach and how long each activity should take.

Cheryl and I discuss improving attendance. We agree this is not going to be easy here. However, I believe the first thing to do is separate parents / guardians into two groups. They are the key to getting children to school. You want to separate parents who do not care about their kid coming to school from those who do not know what to do and say when their child complains about going. I highly recommend picking one day per month and offering one hour informational workshops to parents on a different topic. For example, one might be on what to do when your child says he is too tired to come to school. Another is on what to do when your child threatens you for forcing them to school. I can help with this. Parents who come can be taught exactly what to do and say in each situation. This gives them some feeling of power and control at home. Many want their child to succeed but do not know how to help. As one parent told me a few years ago, "There is no manual that comes with having a child."

The goal here is to get parents and teachers on the same page. This empowers parents to do the right thing because they feel the school supports them. Parents also will meet other parents at the session dealing with the same behavior. They can talk with and consult each other. This is powerful and quickly shows which parents care to get better and which not to waste time with. The second step to improving attendance is for teachers and staff to change their mentality. The negativity is rampant and many are looking for kids to screw up. If I worked here I would walk in every day trying to make the school better than any other place they could be that day. This means I would talk to them, ask questions of kids, praise them, show them that there is a world beyond these hills that maybe someday they can succeed in.

Chapter Twenty
Diffusing Anger in the Moment

Teacher: Jenna Hall, Student: Frank

Ms. Hall asks "How do you diffuse a student that is very upset in the moment?" I teach her my four step process: **Listen, Acknowledge, Agree, Defer.** First listen to what the student is saying. Work really hard at hearing *what* the student is saying and not *how* he is saying it. Then acknowledge what he saying. It sounds like this. "Frank, I hear you." The next step is definitely one of the hardest. Agree. When we agree with someone in this world it is nearly impossible for them to continue arguing. It sounds like this. "Frank, I hear you man and honestly you might even be right." But then immediately *defer* to a later time. "Frank, I hear you and you might be right. But if we try talking about it right now both of us are going to get upset and annoyed and neither of us wants that so I promise I will talk to you about it right after class or later today. Thanks for waiting." Then move. Get out of there both physically and mentally! The goal is always to defer the conversation to a later time if possible. When the later time comes begin the conversation by apologizing to the student about the role you played. "Listen Frank I am sorry. I know we both get fired up which often leads to an argument. I apologize for the part I played and I will work hard not to get upset in the future. Is there anything you think you can do differently next time?" By apologizing I model for him exactly the behavior I want him to show me. I also diffuse any animosity that might still exist from the earlier incident.

Try moving desks into horseshoe or "W" shape. Ms. Hall has them in groups of three with kids staring directly at each other. Not surprisingly she had written a bunch of referrals for talking and disrupting. This formation is like putting a bowl of cocaine in front of an addict and telling them not to snort it. Good luck! If you do not want kids to talk to each other do not have them sitting face to face staring at each other!

I watch the "bell ringer" activity which takes way too long. With just 43 minutes in a period, this activity should not take more than 10 minutes. Try relating the bell ringer to their home lives and make it a relationship building / get to know you better activity instead of always content related. Jenna asks me how to "motivate" a person that does not care about Biology. I ask about the student's home life and once again quickly realize she basically knows nothing about it. I continue to pound the importance of relationship building related to instruction. Teach them life skill lessons needed to survive in this world. I realize this is not in the biology curriculum. Sometimes we have to make a choice.

Chapter Twenty One
Fun in school!

Teacher: Kaitlyn Jones, Students: Whole Class

Your room seems a bit dark. I notice three light bulbs out and shades are down. This is definitely good sometimes. Just be aware of the mood you are trying to create. I love that you introduce me to the class and allow me to get to know your students. This is so important to relationship building and it is obvious you realize this and have strong relationships with your class. When I observe rooms it is very rare the teacher stops and introduces me. I always introduce a stranger to my class. I ask the visitor to talk a little bit about why they are there. Depending on what we are doing that day my students can ask questions of the visitor.

You are teaching about the different coins and the students are engaged and involved. I give you the poem:

Penny penny easy spent copper brown and worth one cent.
Nickel nickel thick and fat you are worth five I know that.
Dime dime little and thin I remember you are worth ten.

Quarter quarter big and bold you are worth 25 I'm told. JFK you make me holler biggest coin worth half a dollar. I like that you have different students come up and point to the coins pictured on white board. Be careful about how they might feel if getting something wrong in front of peers. For certain kids make sure when doing in front of others they get it correct. You have a very friendly personality. Please do not ever lose this!

You are teaching the difference between two digit and one digit numbers. This is fine, but as we discussed, it seems a bit easy for some of them. Never be afraid to push harder academically. With a small class and strong relationships there is more individual attention provided, which means you might be ahead of the curriculum. You have a nice room for only eight students. Be sure to utilize all of it. Maybe create some different sections by using filing cabinets, etc... Students that are ahead (or struggling) can have a place to go within the room and not be distracted. This is a fun room for me to observe and one of the few that incorporates me into what you are doing. I appreciate this!

Chapter Twenty Two
Using Teases to Motivate, Listening to Advice

Teacher: Rebecca Sittel, Students: Whole Class

Your students are arranged in small clusters / groups, except for Andy who is sitting by himself off to the side. You tell me he is not in trouble but he chooses to sit by himself to not get so easily distracted. A few students in the back are working on math while you teach "synonyms" to everyone else. I love your ability to multi task. You tell them to remember the "S." Synonyms = similar. You ask someone to give an example. A little girl says, "Sleep and rest" are similar. You respond, "Yes. Excellent. Great job." Then another boy yells, "Excellent and great" are also synonyms!"

You ask the question, "How come rain falls but clouds do not fall?" They are shouting answers one after another. The class is super excited and desperately wants to know the answer. You say, "Don't worry everyone I am going to tell you the answer, right before lunch!" A huge groan from them. I love it. Whether you know it or not you use a strategy called "Teasing." Our favorite television shows do this to us all the time. They get us super excited and then tell us to tune in next week to see what happens. Great teachers do the same.

I notice the class rules are posted. You tell me kids had a say in creating them. I like the word expectation better than the word rule. An expectation tells a person what to do. A rule tells a person what not to do. Your rule is, "No hitting." An expectation is "we keep our hands and feet to ourselves." I also recommend allowing them a say in the consequence when a rule / expectation is broken. Remember do not predetermine and number your consequences. This can force you to use something that you know will be ineffective because it is on a list. Always use bullet points instead of numbers when creating consequences.

You are naturally a very good question asker. Most teachers tell kids everything. I notice you say all of the following during my 30 minutes in your class. "Which story would you prefer to read? Is there anything I can do to make you feel better about being here because you seem really upset today? If you were me how would you handle the situation? Do you have any ideas for how I can teach this better? I have been harping on questions instead of statements. You do it well.

One thing to be careful of: When we were talking I felt as if it was hard for me to finish a sentence without you immediately telling me you were already doing it or had already tried it. I am often the same way and I need to work on this as well. For me it is my ADHD. I think I know what the person is going to say (and usually I do) so I finish their sentence for them. Be aware of this. It is important as teachers that we really listen. Listening entails asking follow-up questions and allowing people to finish, etc...

We finish by discussing Andy, who might have the worst home life I have ever heard of. His father has been in and out of jail multiple times. His mom is a meth addict. All three siblings, Andy, and their mom live in a mobile home with Grandma. I am told that his father mixed beer with milk in his bottle when Andy was an infant. For a while Andy's dad was constantly on the news as one of the most wanted fugitives in the state. Even with all of this he is one of the smartest kids in the class. The following are bullet points geared toward helping him.

You tell me that Andy gets mad during math. You pinpoint the times he is at his worst. Obviously his home life is a disaster and this is the root of his struggle. It is going to take never ending practice and patience (see Cheryl Corey and Ricky consult on page 82).

- With Andy there are a few phases to improving his behavior. The first is relationship building. You obviously have done this well.
- The second understands how to fill the basic needs he is lacking. Most kids like him are desperate to feel a sense of *power, control, competence, belonging, and attention.* He misbehaves most during Math because he is not good at it. Show him success. Have him do a problem on the board in front of the class. Before he does it, privately give him the correct answer so he gets it right. This will help his confidence. Very rarely give him homework. His homework is called survival. Teach him coping

skills with the crazy life he deals with on a daily basis. I tell the story of a good friend of mine, Marissa. Her father walked out on the family after cheating on her mom when she was five years old. Her mom became both verbally and physically abusive. Because of this Marissa looked to escape. Many kids in this position escape to drugs, alcohol, gangs, or violence. Marissa escaped to books. She locked herself in her room every night and read anything she could get her hands on. Books can be an incredible escape for kids terrified of reality. She was an outstanding student and because of this she now has a master's degree in education. To this day she hates being the center of attention. We both believe this has a lot to do with her childhood.

- The next day ask Andy to do two problems. Give him the answer to one of them and have him do that problem on the board in front of everyone. If he has the second correct (check it before he goes to the board) have him do that one too. If not he just does the first one.
- Remember, this is a progression. During this time ask him to help you write a quiz that the class will take. He can sit with you privately (filling his need for attention) and advise you if the problems are too hard, etc... Continue to always throw in questions, suggestions and comments about improving his disastrous home life.
- These strategies will build his confidence in math, and get him to start believing it is not so bad.
- Outside of class, look for places around the school that he can be a helper.
- Maybe he can be a lunch room monitor or a classroom cleaner. He is desperate to feel a sense of

self-worth. When a person lives a life always being helped they often become helpless. This is a terrible way to go through life. Reverse this by giving him something to be responsible for. I recommend pairing your class up with a local nursing home. Studies show that the loneliest groups of people in the world are kids with no guidance and supervision and old people with no family waiting to die. Putting them together can be powerful.

- Is there a positive male role model you can hook him up with in the school?
- I recommend creating a program where troubled high school kids "adopt" a troubled elementary kid. Or a troubled 2nd grader adopts a troubled kindergartner. This often improves the lives of both students (See Cheryl Corey consult)!
- We discuss his interaction with others during lunch. You point out that most do not like him, which neither of us are surprised about. His social skills are awkward at best. He interrupts and is very physical. I believe all stem from his burning desire for attention. This is also the behavior he sees at home.
- Work with him on these social skills. He must learn how to wait his turn, not interrupt, and most importantly, not come across as so needy to his peers. Practice different scenarios with him.

I have a lot of confidence that you can really help turn him around. Andy is a student to experiment with. Try different strategies. The worst thing that can happen is he remains difficult. Even with all of these ideas his home life is so bad that it will be exceptionally hard for him to succeed. When I have students like this I simply try to focus on making their lives better today than they were yesterday. Changing lives is what we do, even if it is only for a few minutes every day.

Chapter Twenty Three
Teaching Students Where They Are

Teacher: Theo Trist, Student: Ashley

Mr. Trist is in his first year and seems pretty upbeat about his job. The room is small and there is not much space to do labs. I immediately help rearrange the desks from rows into a "W" shape. This is not ideal as he really does need more room. 36 tough kids with one first year teacher seems like an almost impossible task. But he has their attention from the start. He jokes with them, asks about their lives and tells about his.

We discuss a few different kids that he struggles with and I teach him how to focus on the "why" behind each behavior. Without understanding why behaviors occur they are nearly impossible to fix. I use the runny nose example. Pretend you are a doctor and four of your patients have really bad runny noses. You give all of them Kleenex. The runny nose goes away for a bit but all come back the next day because their noses are still running. After a few questions you realize one has allergies and the second is stubborn and refuses to wear a winter hat. The third is a cocaine addict. The symptom you see (runny nose) is the same for all but the solution is very different. Behavior in school is no different. What we see in the classroom from kids (calling out, head down, defiance, etc...) are merely symptoms of something greater. This has been written about multiple times so far.

Mr. Trist then asks what to do with a student that does absolutely nothing. I tell him about my former student, Ashley. It was my second year teaching and my principal Beth came down to my room midway through the year. She looked sad and upset. She said, "Bri I have to let you know that I have a new student for you. Her name is Ashley." Now please understand when teaching self-contained special education and you get a new student midway through the year it is generally not because they have done brilliantly well somewhere else. Usually they have been kicked out thrown out or removed.   Beth (looking down at four pages of notes on her clipboard) then said, "Let me tell you a little bit about Ashley. She has been known to be rude, nasty, defiant, disruptive, uncooperative..." After about 15 adjectives I jumped in.

Me: Are you going to tell me anything good about Ashley?
Beth: (Scanning her sheets up and down), No.
Me: Is she coming anyway?
Her: Yes.
Me: Then I would prefer to find out for myself.

This is a rule I have adopted in my career. Each student in my class gets a fresh slate. It is impossible to do this if I have a ton of information ahead of time. Beth quickly understood this and told me Ashley would be here Monday.

Ashley showed up her first day six minutes late. I was at the door to greet her as she came flying around the corner. She came to a skidding halt about six inches from me. With her arms crossed she looked me up and down about four times and then laughed right in my face. She then got closer (which I didn't realize was possible) and said, "I just wanna let you know I ain't gonna do shit this year. Nothing at all. This school sucks, this class sucks, this room sucks, you suck..." I think she even said the words, "I suck" which would have made no sense. She charged into my room and slammed herself into a desk. The desk actually tipped about half way over. I was kind of hoping it would go all the way over (kidding, sort of). It slammed to the ground and there is Ashley. Now it is my job to teach this kid! Every other student in my class heard exactly what she said. It is not ok for them to think she can talk to me that way. Good thing I used the prevention phrase early in the year, "There are going to be times this year in this classroom that some of you do and say rude, nasty, mean inappropriate things. When that happens I might choose to walk away and keep teaching. It might look to some of you like I am ignoring a behavior. But trust me I am not ignoring it. I just think teaching is more important in that moment." Because I said this I walked directly up to Ashley, looked her right in the eyes, and said, "Nice to meet you too Ashley." Then I got out of there quick! It is so important to say what we need to say and move. Ashley was a kid that literally did absolutely nothing for two weeks. Of course, that year she was at awards night for perfect attendance!

I learned a lot the year I had Ashley. The first thing I learned is that sometimes in a classroom the teacher does not have any good options. Because of this I became really comfortable picking the best of bad options. My best of bad option with Ashley: I would always rather have a student do absolutely nothing at all in my room than nothing at all somewhere else in the building if I see those as my only two options. If I think a student is just going to, "Go to the nurse's office and put their head down" I would rather have their head down in my room. Last I looked when the head is down the ears still work. And I believe I am good enough to say something that will get her interested. This came two weeks later when we were beginning a lesson on Hamlet. I learned early in my career it usually best to try relating content to their lives. I gave them assignment that asked to write about a time in their lives when they deceived someone or were deceived by someone. The next day at the end of class Ashley walked up to me and said, "Mr. Mendler, I did my homework." Before I was able to respond she was gone. I went home that night and began reading the papers. I read Ben's paper first. He was with me the entire year and his paper was very good. Then I got to Ashley's. I wish I knew at the time I would be writing books and teaching workshops because I would have saved her paper. It was the most incredible thing I have ever read. It said this:

Deceivedbyashley

There was a time in my life I was deceived it was by my boyfriend we were at a party
I was like yo what's up with that other girl
He was like yo I don't know
I was like yo what do you mean you don't know

He was like yo I said I don't know….

For two straight pages I read, "I was like yo he was like yo I was like yo." I am not exaggerating when I tell you I got done reading the paper and I was like YO! It was the absolute worst paper I have ever read. I am not sure if you have ever gotten an assignment from a student where at first you are super excited to get it, but then totally overwhelmed with where to begin. The question I ask people to think about: If I grade Ashley's paper the way most teachers do, by comparing it to Ben's paper, what grade do I have to give it? Many of you will say, "F." Some of you nicer teachers might say, "D" or C- but with the long minus. That is true. But really think about this. If I grade Ashley's paper by comparing it to her own previous work, what grade do I have to give Ashley's paper? It is 100% better than anything else she has done for me all year! Which is more likely to get Ashley to do the next assignment? Ashley was an easy one. She told me on her first day of school that she hated my class and sucked at it. So why don't I give her an "F" and confirm everything she already believes about English? This is what I like to call the number one motivation killer of kids in school. The number one motivation killer is this: They do the best job on assignment that they know how to do and we tell them it stinks. I am going to say that again. They do the best job on an assignment that they can possibly do in that moment, and we tell them it is awful! I did not fall into this trap. Everyone in my room gets an "A" on their first assignment.

The next day Ashley got her paper back and waited after class to talk to me. Without warning she said, "Do you think I am stupid or something?" To which I replied, "Yes, Very (JOKING)." I said, "No Ashley why would you say that?

Her: Mr. Mendler, do you know how old I am?

Me: 16 or 17?

Her: I am 17 years old. And just so you know I have never once gotten an "A" on anything in my life. This paper ain't no "A" because I know an "A" when I see one. So change it. In that moment I learned she was honest. This girl is not going to steal from me. My best students never tell me their grade is too high!

Me: You lucked out this year!

Her: Why

Me: Because you got me for a teacher and you never had a teacher like me. Everyone in this class starts off with an "A." You can ask everyone else but they might not remember because it was back in September. Has anyone ever taught you how to write a sentence, because it does not really look like it.

Her: Not really.

Me: A sentence is a subject and a verb. Ashley runs. That is a sentence.

Her: No it is not.

Me: Yes it is.

Her: How come they are so long in books and stuff?

Me: Because there are ways to write much better sentences and we will get there. But tonight your homework is to write three perfect sentences. And if her sentences are perfect her grade is an "A" again. But they were not perfect. This is how low functioning a student she was. An 11th grader who cannot write three perfect sentences with two words!

Of course, I was thinking the same thing many of you probably are. So I asked my principal, "How did she get this far?"

Beth: Go ahead and ask me that again.

Me: Ok how did she get this far?

Beth: One last time ask me that question.

Me: How did she get this far?

Beth (raising her voice a bit): Don't ever ask that question again!!!! That is the stupidest question a person could possibly ask!!! How do I know how she got this far!?!?!? But here she is! She is this far. So you can complain that she should not be here or you can go down there and get her. And believe me Brian, She is way down there so you are going to have to pull hard to get her up!

I said ok. I'm going down to get her.

To take you through the next two months in a few sentences:

Me: Has anyone shown you how to write a paragraph? Because a paragraph is just three or four sentences put together around one topic sentence. So tonight your homework is to write one perfect paragraph. Then two, three and four. In the middle of May I point up to a white board in my room that never changes. It has the dates June 21st and 22nd written on it.

Me: You know what these are the dates of?

Her: No.

Me: The New York State Regents Exam that you will pass.

Her: No I won't.

Me: Why not?

Her: Remember what I told you a few months ago about never getting an "A" on anything in my life?

Me: I remember.

Her: I've never passed a test in my life. I am always the kid who fails. I don't know how to pass tests.

Me: You lucked out this year!

Her: Why

Me: Because you got me for a teacher and you have never had a teacher like me! I don't care what the idiots in Albany,

NY tell you it is not possible for you to fail. Look at what you handed me six months ago (I was like yo he was like yo I was like yo). Last night you handed me four perfect paragraphs. You are not a failure. Remember, attitude and effort are the only two things in life people can control. You have done fantastic with both.

Then we crammed for the test. I taught her to use the words metaphor, personification, alliteration, and simile. It does not necessarily matter if she uses them correctly. Just put them in your essay. She took the test and failed by two points. I try hard not to get emotionally tied to a student's test score but I must admit I wanted this one really badly! Ashley went to summer school and made up the two months she missed with us (remember she came in November) and passed the second time. What I can tell you about Ashley is if you asked her today what her best subject was in 11th grade, she would have told you English. With all due respect she stunk at English. But she believed she was good. In school this is half the battle. Kids must believe they can succeed at something before they will give maximum effort. Of course we know this in every other aspect of life. The first baseball league our kids play in is called T-Ball. Because we know success of bat hitting ball comes first. Almost always we use training wheels when teaching to ride a bike. The goal is for the child to feel what it is like to pedal. Then there is a progression to no training wheels but the parent holds onto the seat. Eventually the child is riding all over the neighborhood.

The moral of this story is give kids hope and they will almost always show you effort. Once there is effort success pops in. Once success comes confidence takes over and the amazing cycle begins. Compare students to themselves in school and great things happen. Make the competition being better today than they were yesterday. "Yesterday you called out inappropriately six times. Today needs to be five or less. Yesterday you got out of your seat five times today do you think it can be four or less?"

Chapter Twenty Four
Stop Being Boring!

Teacher: Geoff Taylor, Students: Whole Class

I spend an entire 40 minutes observing the disaster that is Mr. Taylor's social studies class. He reads a power point slide by slide to 34 students in a cramped room. It reminds me of Wonder Years Ben Stein (anyone, anyone). At first the kids are chatty but not horrible. Within 10 minutes the room turns into a free for all. Taylor talks about slavery and the civil war. It is very hard to hear him as his voice is very soft. I am not saying we need to yell but a little bit of energy would be wonderful. These are two topics that should be interesting if taught correctly. Why is the Civil War important to their lives? Feel free to look up from the power point for one second and ask a question! Talk to the people in front of you! Out of 34 two pay attention. 14 straight minutes and he has not looked up. Not once. It is kind of comical that a person can be this oblivious to the mess around them.

To this point there is no relating content to student lives. This is very important and is discussed with him during my meeting next period. He literally just reads the slides one after another. No question asking and three students have their heads down the entire time. At least they are not disrupting! About 20 minutes in I notice an aid in the room. I didn't see her because she was sitting at a desk (like a student) the entire class. I am not really sure what her role is or why she is here. There is no detailed agenda written on the board.

He then introduces a writing assignment that has absolutely nothing to do with Social Studies or anything else he is talking about. This is a disaster. It is all I can do to not jump up and take over. The essay topic is about following directions, and how to walk into class. I am confused as to why you assign this nine weeks into the school year? I am guessing they still need work on these skills. But why write about them? Just practice. Class mercifully ends.

During our consult I spend a lot of time showing him how to specifically connect content to kids and their lives. Ask them, "How many of you are in a gang or know someone who is?" Talk to them about protecting home turf and their neighborhood and standing up for what is right. Then connect this to the civil war. Many of these kids are fighting their own wars every day.

I recommend eliminating power point for one week. He resists. I explain the two equal parts necessary to be a good teacher, content and kids. Fortunately he knows the content very well. The next step is to become interesting, exciting and entertaining while teaching. Go online and search for interesting lessons that relate to tough inner city kids. Talk to them about their lives. Ask questions and then ask follow up questions. Instead of focusing on teaching Social Studies, focus on teaching people.

I recommend showing good, high quality videos instead of reading power points. These kids are conditioned to watch television when they go home. Because their brains are already wired this way, showing movies and videos will be very beneficial. I also inquire about the essay topic choice. My recommendation is that any essay topic should either get them learning content or the teacher learning about kids. Since the class is history, maybe the topic is: "How they got to Texas," or "Where my family is from." You do the essay as well so they can learn about their teacher. Just about anything is a better topic than the one he chose.

The other problem with Mr. Taylor is that he is a total nerd. His hair is a mess, his shirt is wrinkled and he wears a strange bow tie. His pants are about a foot too short and his socks are mismatched (no big deal except you can see them while he is standing). It is important to look the part. I am not saying teachers need to spend thousands of dollars on a wardrobe. But if you want to build relationships with middle or high school kids a little bit of style is necessary.

Chapter Twenty Five
Start with your Best!

Teacher: Colleen Pituala, Students: Whole class

The whole class gathers around on the carpet toward the front of the room. You tell them to "tip toe to the carpet," but it takes way too long. In fact, just about everything takes too long. If you wait for every kid to be perfectly quiet and ready before you start you will never start! Sometimes picking up the pace will greatly help you with classroom management. Keep things moving!

Rug space is very crowded and it is not surprising kids are touching and messing with each other. She asks a student publicly what is wrong and gets no answer. I believe I have mentioned the word privacy about 50 times thus far. The lesson is on the days of the week. It literally takes 10 minutes for a student to say, "Today is Wednesday September 11th." This is a perfect time to make reference to 9/11. Maybe ask a question like, "So can anyone tell me why this day is extremely important in American History?" Or, "Can anyone tell me what happened X years ago today?"

Try tying the event into the lesson you are already doing! 9/11 is not even mentioned.

A couple of students are disruptive and you ask them to go back to their seats. I am not surprised they are disruptive, as again, the lesson is taking way too long and the space is way too crowded. Finally she does a really cool song about the days of the week. Every student is participating and paying attention. Even the two that were sent back to their seats are participating. Why not start with this? Everything else can play off of the song. I believe in starting with your best stuff. It is so hard to hook them as it is. I also explain that it is important to forgive. When students are sent back to their seats they should be allowed back to the activity as soon as they are ready to participate. There is no need to hold any grudge. Forgive, forget, and move on. When kids are participating my rule is I never make them stop no matter what happened earlier in the day.

Chapter Twenty Six
Maybe you are in the Wrong Profession

Teacher: Kaitlyn Van, Students: Whole Class

You seem miserable. I am in the room for 20 minutes and you do not smile once. You said to a student, "You can sit there until you learn how to use your manners because you have none!" This was said condescendingly and in front of others. Sadly none flinch which lets me believe this is normal dialogue here. Unless the chair has some magical teaching power, I am not sure how "sitting there" is going to teach him manners. How about you spend some time teaching them? We must model the behavior we want to see from them.

I count six students with their hands properly raised to ask a question and all are completely ignored. Why? What are you trying to prove? You are not a dictator. This is a classroom. We are supposed to be nice to kids. This is the most basic aspect of our job! You tell me you do not like when kids "call out your name." I tell you that each student who called your name first raised their hand and was completely ignored. What do you expect? Three times you tell kids what you "need them" to do. If they cared what you needed they would have already done it! How about using "please" or "thank you?"

I am shocked and saddened at the lack of empathy you show toward your class. The militaristic approach you take does not work. The good news is if you do the complete opposite of what you are doing now you might have some level of success. Go out of your way to make kids feel good. When you are asked a question it is ok to answer with a smile. Compassion, caring, fun, and loving are all adjectives that describe teachers with strong classroom management. Work at becoming these if possible. If not, I highly recommend finding another profession. Nobody should have to spend five hours / 180 days with this level of misery. I spend 20 minutes in here and cannot wait to get out.

Chapter Twenty Seven
Teaching and Using Manners

Teacher: Feliz Ogbaama, Students: Whole class

B e careful turning your back on kids. Try hard to position yourself at a point of the room where you can see everyone at all times. If this is not possible get some small mirrors and strategically place them around your room. This literally gives eyes in the back of your head.

Kids here need to be taught manners. Teachers should demand "please" and "thank you" every time. "Yo Miss O let me get a pencil" is not the proper way to talk to a teacher. Ask him to ask again. This time say, "Miss O, may I please borrow a pencil?" After you give it make sure he says thank you. If he does not say thank you take the pencil back until he does. This works both ways. Be sure you always use manners when asking them to do something.

Praise privately. I cannot stress this enough. I model for her exactly how to praise kids. For example, they are expected to walk in perfectly straight, silent lines. Most do it extremely well. You wouldn't know that by walking down the hall. The focus is on the one or two not doing the right thing. Say, "Great job, I love how you are walking, well done. I am proud of you guys. Awesome line. Keep it up." Then privately go to the one and say, "Young lady please stop talking in the hall." Praise more than you correct! During my time in your room I count seven different directions to students without saying please or thank you. It is amazing how teachers often do not use the very manners we expect from our students. She asks a student to read out loud to the class. When that student finishes another starts reading. I am not a huge fan of this. I prefer the teacher read out loud to them. This way everyone is at the same place and you know exactly where that place is. I give her many of the same suggestions I give the others. Praise, positivity, privacy, manners, and modeling the behaviors you want to see from your students.

Chapter Twenty Eight
My Special Ed. Model

Throughout this book I referenced how I "didn't like the way special education was done" in certain places. I am an enormous believer in departmentalizing Middle and High School SPED teachers. The thought is always to give SPED teachers as few content areas to focus on, and as many different kids as possible to teach. This means each teaches some ED (Emotionally Disturbed), some MC (Mentally Challenged), some inclusion, and some LD (Learning Disabled). They will probably do some resource room as well, but hopefully only focusing on one content. If a school has five SPED teachers in grades 5-8 and five teacher aides, a hypothetical schedule looks like this:

Hypothetical SPED Math Schedule: Teacher 1

Period 1	Inclusion 7th grade math
Period 2	Self-contained 7th grade ED/LD math
Period 3	7/8 MC Self-contained Math
Period 4	Inclusion 5 or 6 Math
Period 5	Self-contained 5/6 ED Math

Period 6	Inclusion 8th grade Math
Period 7	Self-contained 8th grade ED/LD Math
Period 8	Math skills (or possibly an elective with SPED kids)
Period 9	Free Period

Hypothetical SPED Science Schedule:

Period 1	Self-contained 7th grade ED Science
Period 2	Inclusion 7th grade Science
Period 3	Inclusion 5/6 Science
Period 4	7/8 MC Self-contained Science
Period 5	Inclusion 8th grade Science
Period 6	Self-contained 5/6 ED Science
Period 7	Self-contained 8th grade Science
Period 8	Free Period
Period 9	Science skills

Reasons this is a better model:

- **Test scores increase for everyone involved.**
  Suppose a Gen Ed teacher needs three days off for some reason. Now the SPED teacher can easily fill in and teach that content because they are a content expert. The level of instruction does not drop off.
- **Self-contained kids finally get the education they deserve**. These kids deserve equal or even better instruction than their gen ed. peers, yet the way many programs are created the instruction is worse. This is not usually the teachers fault, as many are placed in an unrealistic situation that requires teaching multiple content areas to multiple grade level students all at the same time. The good Lord himself could not accomplish this!

- **Across the board better behavior.** A major key to good behavior is a strong lesson. The lessons will be stronger in inclusion and self-contained settings. This is the point to doing the new model.
- **True "Inclusion" can happen** because the SPED teacher becomes a content expert, and is viewed as such by all gen ed. kids and gen ed. teachers.
- **SPED teacher attends specific content department meetings** and becomes immersed in one content area like their gen ed. colleagues (Hence more content expertise).
- **Self-contained kids switch classes and rooms**, but remain with a small group led by a content expert SPED teacher. For those who struggle with transitions this is helpful as the only way to get better at something is to do MORE of it. Plus self-contained kids now switch classes which make them feel like real middle and high school students. Since the SPED teacher does inclusion in the same content area the stigma of being a SPED kid almost always goes away.
- **Inclusion SPED teachers are much more able to help** any student as they are working with the same content all day.
- **All SPED teachers work with all types of SPED kids during the day.** This keeps all of them versatile and fresh in case you need to eliminate a position or add a position in the future.
- **Instead of having extremely challenging kids all day teachers only have them for one block or period**. This is much more manageable for everyone.
- **SPED teachers can now better collaborate** with each other as they teach the same kids during different blocks.

- **This tremendously helps future inclusion classes**. The second year working together a SPED teacher can immediately fill in a gen ed. teacher on strategies, techniques, and ideas that worked the previous year in that specific content area for a particular student. Again, the teacher is teaching only that content.
- **No more free rides for SPED teachers.** Under this model administrators can truly evaluate their SPED teachers. Some SPED Inclusion teachers have easy jobs as the SPED inclusion kids are well behaved AND they are not required to be the main content expert. They become a highly paid glorified aide.
- **Easier to evaluate self-contained teachers**. Self-contained teacher evaluation scores from administrators are usually much lower than any other SPED teacher. This is because their job is much more challenging. Under this model all teachers are evaluated equally, which in this case is fair. Now all SPED teachers can be evaluated in either self-contained or inclusion classes as they all do both during the day.

Possible downsides to this:
- One I hear is that teachers cannot build relationships as strongly because they are not with the same kids all day. I see this argument but do not agree with it, and it certainly does not outweigh 14 reasons the other model is better.
- Consistency for inclusion SPED kids. Some people argue that having the same SPED teacher with the same kids all day is better. Again I disagree. I think having four or five different SPED teachers that are experts in individual content areas is much better.

- Some SPED teachers will complain. Right now there are some teachers that have really easy jobs. They do not have to work with any challenging kids all day. Some of them might complain. Big deal. The focus is on doing what is best for kids. Right?

The first step is for everyone to agree this is a much better model. Some places I work this happens quickly. Other places refuse to see anything different from what they already do.

Once agreed the next step is to re-look at all SPED people and how they are utilized. It is also best to ask each teacher and aide to rank their favorite / best content area to their least favorite / weakest content area. A teacher might not get her first choice but almost definitely will not get her last choice either. The goal is to put people in the content area . they like best.

Conclusion

Dan was the toughest kid I ever taught and the day he threw me on the desk was my most challenging day as a teacher. However, I continued to believe in him. I continue believe in all kids because that is my nature. I continue to believe in all kids because without that belief I have no chance at being successful. I continue to believe in all kids because I do not believe the hand they are dealt is their fault. If I can change one child the world will be a better place.

Now it is your turn. I cannot do it for you. I can lead you there, but now you have to decide. How are you going to be remembered five years from now? Stop worrying about what the lady down the hall is doing or the guy next door. At the end of the day it is 30-35 kids and you, the ultimate challenge. Embrace it, enjoy it, and remember you always control your attitude and your effort. I am grateful for all you do for our children. Do not ever give up on **THAT ONE KID**!